...rrr...

Book of the Biza

rrre

Compiled by Ashok Malik

Lustre Press
Roli Books

Contents

Introduction

bizarre /bɪ'zɑː/ ▸ adj. very strange or unusual

We live in a prosaic and essentially un-heroic age. So many of the dark secrets, evocative mysteries and eerie phenomena of the past centuries, which troubled and puzzled humankind till as recently as the early twentieth century, have been resolved. The gaps on the map of the world have been filled; the moon has been conquered; there is no need, and no stomach, for adventurers who made the age of discovery and exploration their golden hour. When we know too much perhaps we celebrate too little. The thirst for knowledge has been replaced by a surfeit of information. It all seems commonplace – it all seems much *less* bizarre.

This book started off, therefore, as a challenge: to identify enough contemporary phenomena that remain bizarre. The word was defined in the broadest sense, to mean strange occurrences, eerie coincidences, interesting correlations, unusual social or even national habits and responses, extraordinary battles or contests, oddball characters, unexplained mysteries (of which there are, alas, too few in our world).

There was little point in re-telling history's bizarre stories and simply recounting conspiracy theories and conundrums from, say, 500 years ago. To make an impact, the list had to be relevant to today's reader. That is why no episode, incident or occurrence in this book can be dated back further than about 150 years. The mid-nineteenth century, the cusp of the modern age if we could so term it, is where our endeavours begin.

The roots of the globalization era that we are living in go back to about that time. The first spell of globalization was the imperial age. Like globalization, but openly and overtly so, imperialism was a gigantic social engineering project. A clutch of western powers sought to reshape the world in their image. In the process, they effaced localized customs – some iniquitous and unhealthy, others merely quirky – that could have qualified as bizarre by a contemporary reckoning.

Some of these survived into the twentieth century, and are part of the following pages. The battle against cannibalism, for instance, was as much a product of the Enlightenment as its twin, the Age of Imperialism. Yet, till as recently as the 1950s, a secluded community in New Guinea was suffering from debilitating disease because of the practice of eating human flesh. It was only increased and intensive engagement with the external world that gradually changed menus and mores.

Globalization follows a similar trajectory but the driving force is the market, not munitions. As we evolve into the proverbial global village, with shared values, business systems, cultural products, tastes, urban landscapes, even architecture, aesthetics and design, in a sense we are all becoming conformists. The space for the zany eccentric is contracting.

What this means is that the task of putting together a collection of the bizarre is that much more difficult. Twenty years from now, if some intrepid publisher commissions an author to write the story of bizarre phenomena of the twenty-first century, I suspect the book will take a long, long time to cook.

What may save us – if indeed a fetish for the bizarre merits saving! – is the human imagination. Among the stories in this book are those of incredulousness – of a community's or entire society's belief in an idea that may appear to others as nonsensical; there is cultism and exotic ritualism; there is, at times, unexplained premonition and coincidence, which science and rationalism cannot quite explain, and which tests mortal frontiers.

These are notions and concepts that have influenced civilization since the time ancient man began his quest for the lost continent of Atlantis. Today, it exists in a million sites on the internet, which navigate the hidden worlds of our minds, of our fears and hopes, our internal superstitions and our external failures, our carefully hidden instinct and our carelessly placed trust – and our taste for the bizarre.

Enjoy the book; I hope it helps you savour this world. It's a strange, unusual, crazy, decidedly imperfect and downright bizarre world – but it's the only one we have.

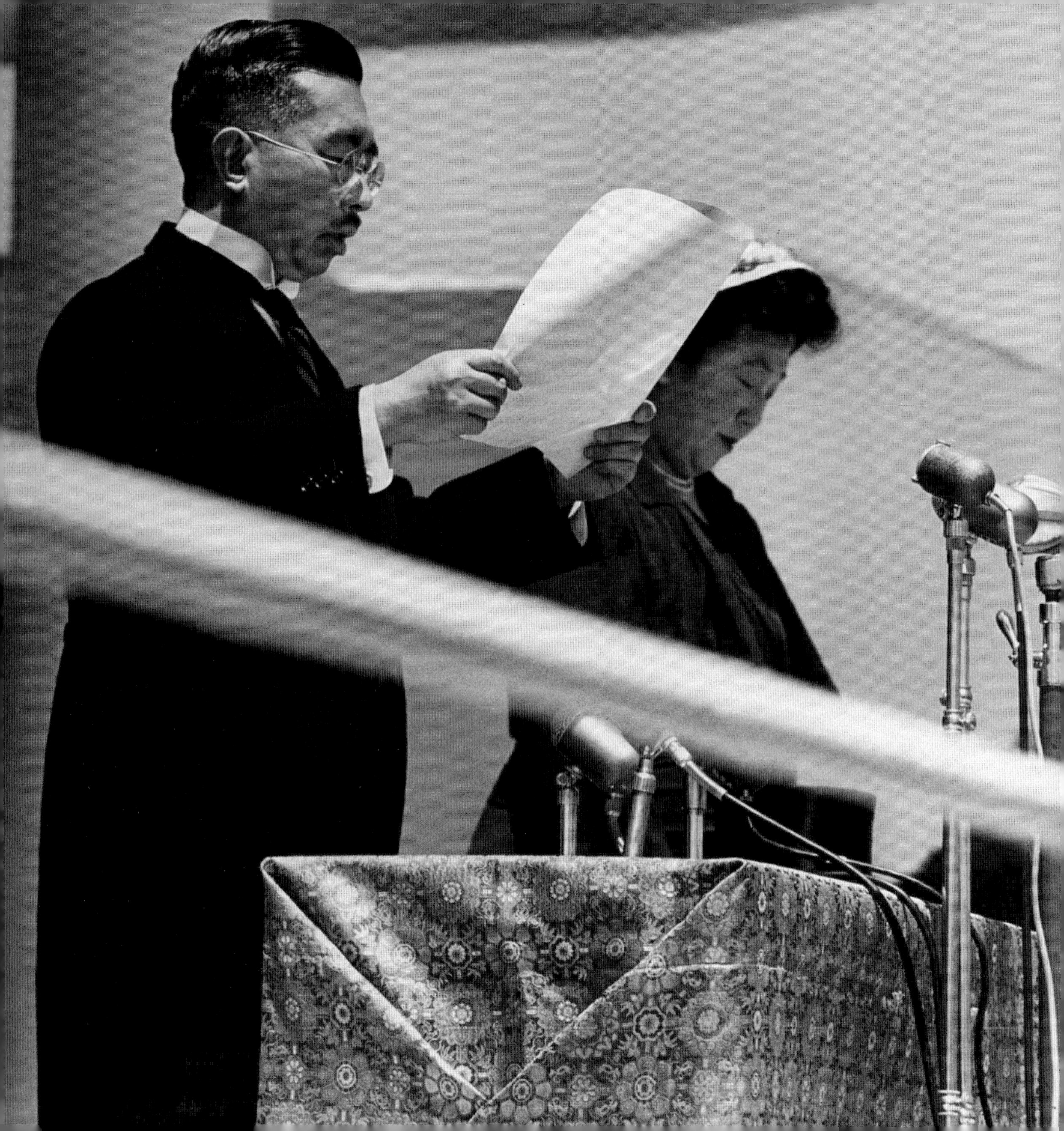

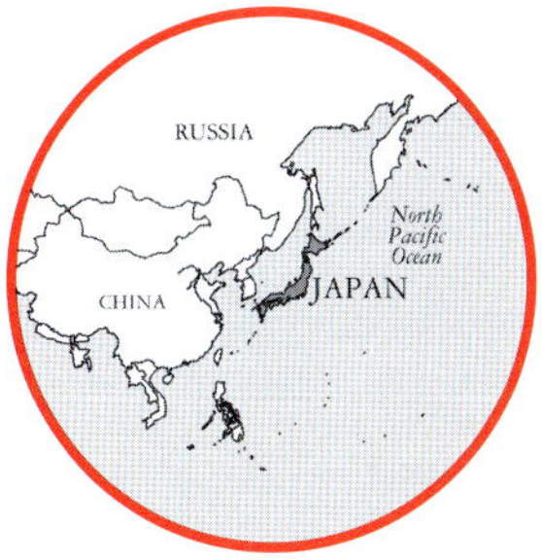

God insists he's only human

On 1 January 1946, a marine biologist four months short of his forty-fifth birthday got up and made a radio broadcast, insisting he was not God. It wasn't another crank comedy show; to Japan, it was serious business, a life-altering experience. Emperor Hirohito, ruler of the Asian industrial and military power that had just been defeated by the Allies in World War II, told his people to reject the 'false conceptions that the emperor is divine'. He was as human as the next person.

For centuries, the people of Japan had held a contrary belief. Shinto, the indigenous faith that saw Japan as, in essence, God's chosen country, decreed that the ruling family

Kimono clad Japanese kneeling and bowing to the emperor as he enters their quarters.

FACING PAGE: Emperor Hirohito reading a speech, in which he pledged to embrace democracy, before a gathering of 15, 000 people at the Imperial Plaza during celebrations of Japan's restored sovereignty on 3 May, 1952.

was descended from Amaterasu, the sun-goddess and fairy godmother of Japan. Not only was the emperor divine, he was absolute. You lived for him and died with him, literally.

In 1912, when Hirohito's grandfather, the Emperor Meiji died, the country's best-known general committed suicide as did his (the general's) wife. The event must have left an impact on Hirohito: the general was his tutor.

Hirohito's renunciation of divinity – 'he has to de-god himself,' said the typically irreverent American soldiers in Japan – shook his society. It had lost three million men and women, soldiers and civilians, in World War II. It was physically battered, psychologically wounded. When its god-emperor declared his mortality, the moral compass went awry.

Innumerable suicides were reported as a whole nation woke up to, in a sense, rationalism. Japan's rebirth had begun – as all births are bound to – painfully. In its first decade under an acknowledged human emperor, it laid the foundations of a spectacular technological and economic boom.

Japanese warrior takes leave of his family to kill himself on the death of his Lord, colour illustration circa 1900.

Disease for man-eaters

It is the world's strangest disease. The symptoms are severe mood swings, laughing fits, lack of coordination, tremors and slurred speech. In weeks, the patient is unable to eat or stand. In less than a year he is dead.

This is the curse of Kuru, a killing disorder that atrophies the brain. It is a disease so rare that it is found only among the Fore tribals in the mountainous rainforests of Papua New Guinea. Kuru is passed on by a most eerie carrier – the human brain tissue. Its only victims are (were) cannibals: those Fore tribals who ate the brain of a dead human being contracted the disease and unsuspectingly waited for it to incubate in their bodies. The incubation could take years and hence nobody made the connection till Australian medical investigators arrived in the 1950s. They were puzzled by the fatal laughing sickness of Papua New Guinea. The truth was, if you forgive the pun, unwholesome.

Kuru belongs to a family of infectious diseases called transmissible spongiform encephalopathies. A sister is the Mad Cow Disease among cattle. Kuru destroys the brain, reduces it to pulp as it were, slowly but remorselessly. Day by day, hour by hour, the victim loses that much more of his cogitative faculties. Today, Kuru has almost vanished from Papua New Guinea.

Not because a cure has been found, but because the government has stepped in to stop the tribal wars that ended in cannibalistic feasts.

FACING PAGE: Males of Papua, about to indulge in their evening meal with chopsticks as their spoons. Ritualized cannibalism led to the spread of Kuru, prompting the Australian administration to outlaw the practice in 1959.

9/11: Pentagon attacked on birthday

One of the abiding mysteries of our time is the question of why the Al-Qaeda terrorists chose September 11 as the date, in 2001, on which to attack the United States. Where there are mysteries, there are conspiracy theories and extraordinary coincidences. September 11 was rich in significance for the Pentagon and New York City, location of the World Trade Center.

On 11 September 1941, the groundbreaking ceremony of the new office of the United States Defence Department, just outside Washington D.C. took place. In other words, it was the day on which the foundation of the Pentagon was laid. In a sense, the twenty-nine-acre building – once called the world's largest office complex – was marking its sixtieth birthday on 9/11, when a hijacked plane smashed into it.

FACING PAGE: A 1947 aerial view of the Pentagon, headquarters of the United States Department of Defense, believed to be the largest 'office' in the world.

For Manhattan island, where the Twin Towers stood out as a modern marvel, 9/11 also marked an inaugural anniversary. On 11 September 1609, explorer Henry Hudson sailed into, what is today, New York Harbour and became the first white man to set foot on Manhattan.

Did the terrorists know of these dates? Speculation was rife in those tempestuous days following 9/11 that the date was actually linked to the massacre of Israeli athletes by Palestinian terrorists in 1972. That horror had convulsed the Munich Olympics, leading to a sombre conclusion of the Games on 11 September 1972.

Those with longer memories delved deeper. In history's great clash between West and East, between Christian and Islamic civilizations, the Battle of Vienna that began two hours before dawn on the night of 11–12 September 1683 was momentous. It saw a Polish-Austrian alliance vanquish the invading Turks. The Ottoman Empire was crippled. Islam's march to the West finally, and definitively, halted.

A full 318 years later, was Osama bin Laden extracting vengeance?

Maybe he'd only read a book most others had missed. Twenty years before 9/11, American Ernest L. Martin wrote a book called 'The Birth of Christ Recalculated'. Later republished as 'The Star that Astonished the World', it sought to marry astronomy to religious belief; to arrive at a date for the astral conjunction said to have marked Christ's birth. Martin's date for Jesus' birthday was – 11 September 3 BC.

An aerial view of the west side of the Pentagon destroyed by the crash of an American Airlines aircraft in 2001.

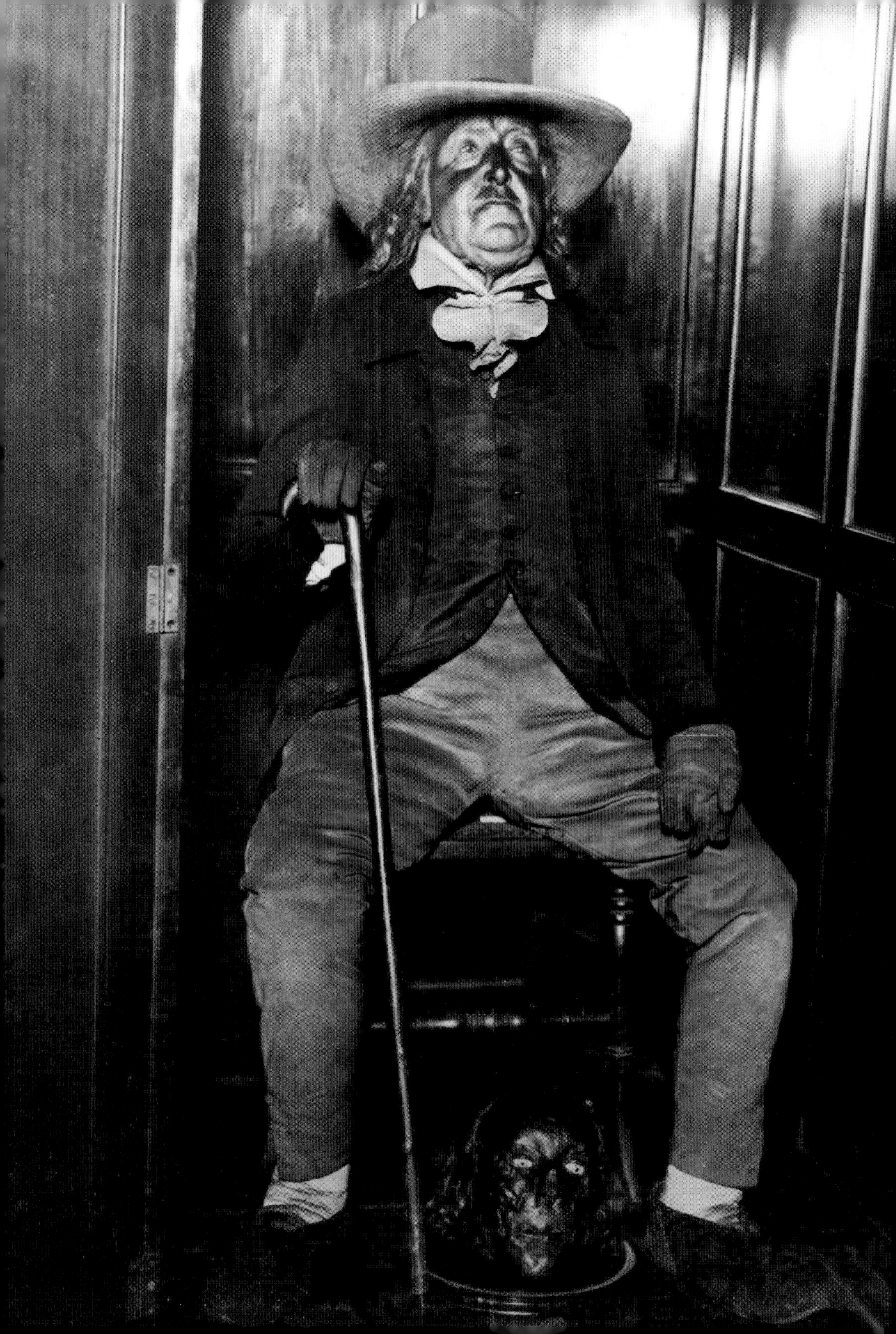

The Auto Icon of Jeremy Bentham at the University College, London. His real head (below, near feet), was badly disfigured but displayed in the same case for many years.

Dead man in attendance

At the end of a hallway in the main building of the University College of London, is a large wooden cabinet with a glass front. Within the cabinet sits a most singular resident – the Auto Icon. This is the skeleton of Jeremy Bentham (1748–1832): philosopher, political thinker, and an early benefactor of the institution that now surrounds him.

The skeleton wears Bentham's clothes, right down (or up!) to his hat, and holds his walking stick. A wax reproduction of his head crowns, as it were, the skeleton. Bentham's real head was rendered unusable when, after his death, it was disfigured during a flawed mummification attempt. For years, the real head lay near the legs of the Auto Icon. More than once it was stolen and found at places as far apart as a railway station and a football field. Finally, the head was removed to the University College's vault.

Why is Bentham still alive, even in death? He willed so, desiring his reincarnation into the Auto Icon for, the legend goes, he wished to be present at every meeting of the College Council till the end of time.

The control freak may have had a nobler goal too. Bentham was among the foremost advocates of the legal use of dead bodies for dissection. He felt that this would further medical science. As the Auto Icon – a name he coined himself – he felt he could help in a form his contemporaries may not even have realized. Certainly, he's done his bit as an object of black curiosity.

ROCK"N"ROLL
MASSIMO
JIM MORRISON
CATANIA
ROSAN
JIM
MORRISON

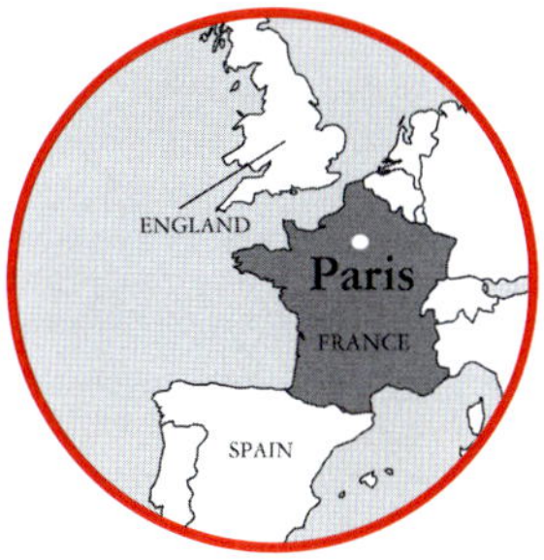

Disturbing the peace

Ever visited the world's most disturbed grave? When Jim Morrison, lead guitarist and vocalist of The Doors and iconic symbol of the rebellious 1960s, died in 1971, he was buried at Paris's majestic and serene Le Pere Lachaise cemetery. With the rock star around at the cemetery, life (or death, if you prefer) could never be the same. A private corner became an international tourist hotspot.

Every year, a million and a half visitors arrive at Le Pere Lachaise. A vast majority of them come to see Morrison's grave, even though they may not be fans of The Doors. There are all sorts of them: ageing hippies, trendy teens, Americans and Asians, baby boomers and bohemians. They leave behind a whole host of gifts for the rock star who will forever be remembered as the boyish twenty-seven-year-old he was when he died. You will see flowers at Morrison's grave, apart from wine bottles, guitars and photographs.

FACING PAGE: The grave of Jim Morrison as it looked in 1986. Some years later the bust got stolen, after which the French authorities cleaned up all the graffiti and posted a policeman there.

For years, as grieving relatives of those buried nearby stared in horror, Morrison's final resting place had become a gigantic ashtray. Graffiti, trash, and broken bottles lay strewn around. In 1997, the French authorities scrubbed the grave and its surroundings, and placed a guard round the clock. In fact, Morrison's monument was even seen as a potential terrorist target.

The after-life for Morrison is a little calmer today. Yet, come 3 July, his death anniversary, and new generations of fans arrive in their thousands. In 1991 a riot had broken out at Le Pere Lachaise, with the police having to use teargas.

A monument is often greater than the sum of its parts, acquiring a resonance beyond the immediate. To be fair, this is so with the grave of Jim Morrison too. To his fans, it is not just a cult singer who is buried there, but the entire ethos; the rebelliousness, the recklessness and free-spirited fervour of the sixties.

The man who called himself the 'Lizard King', naturally attracts the world's eccentrics and drifters to his final home. One photographer, an American who moved to Paris, took photographs of Morrison's tombstone almost everyday between 1989 and 1994. Another crafted a white bust and left it at the grave.

One follower called Morrison's grave the 'Alternative Arlington', a reference to the resting place of American war heroes and other symbols of courage. Not bad for a man who didn't live to be thirty and thought of himself as an imperfect poet.

Morrison's death was one part the triple 'J' tragedy of 1970–71. In a ten-month period between September 1970 and July 1971, Jimi Hendrix, Janis Joplin and Jim Morrison, three icons of the Beatnik generation, dropped out from the planet, victims of the excesses of youth. The Sixties was over; the counter-culture was officially dead. It lies buried along with a musical genius in an otherwise quiet neighbourhood in Paris.

A fan lays flowers on Jim Morrison's grave, on the anniversary of the singer's 50th birthday in 1993. Morrison, lead singer for the rock group 'The Doors', died on 3 July 1971.

Inspiring the inspiration

What links a thirteenth-century trading centre in Western Europe to a nineteenth-century court in eastern India? The destinies of Ypres and Calcutta are two worlds united by architecture.

By the end of the twelfth century, Ypres, a small town in what is today the Flemish part of Belgium, was beginning to establish itself as a bustling location for the cloth trade. Between 1250 and 1304, it built itself the Gothic-style Lakenhalle (Cloth Hall) to facilitate its major industry. The Lakenhalle became the economic focus of the town. Its political status was institutionalized when the building's eastern end was added in the early seventeenth century, as the Stadhuis or Town Hall.

In the late nineteenth century, the British sought to build a grand high court in Calcutta. Walter Granville, assigned the job of designing the building, painstakingly reproduced the Gothic structure and imposing tower of the Ypres Stadhuis. In 1872, the mimic Lakenhalle was inaugurated.

FACING PAGE: 1st July 1922: Pilgrims in Cloth Hall, Ypres, after the town was completely destroyed in World War I.

Forty years later Europe was at war, and Ypres was in the thick of it. The Flemish front was a bitterly contested theatre of World War I. Over 550,000 soldiers died here between 1914 and 1918. Ypres itself was shelled and bombed out of existence. The devastation was complete; the beloved Cloth Hall remained only in dreams and memories.

When the war ended, the people of Ypres resolved to rebuild their city. The Lakenhalle, it was decided, had to look just the way it had for seven centuries. Its reconstruction would be a testimony to the city's resilience.

The problem was the original building plans – the blueprints for the Lakenhalle/Stadhuis had disappeared.

There was no reference point for architects to begin their work. An SOS went out to Calcutta. A copy of the building plans of the high court was sought and studied. The job of re-conjuring the pride of Ypres began.

By 1962, the new Lakenhalle was ready. It had taken a long time – forty-four years since the Great War ended. What was four decades, however, for a story that had begun in about AD 1200 and travelled halfway across the world?

ABOVE: The Calcutta High Court, built in 1862, is an exact replica of the Cloth Hall in Ypres, Belgium.

FACING PAGE: The rebuilt Town Hall which was completed in 1962, bearing a strong resemblance to its Indian counterpart.

Cult without a prophet

Religious fringe groups are born of peculiar, even eccentric, principles and beliefs. Few are stranger than the Rastafarian cult, which arose in Jamaica in the 1920s. It combined a sort of 'Black power' movement with Biblical allusions, drawing from the Old Testament to establish that Ethiopia was the homeland of the Black man and, indeed, of all mankind.

The Book of Genesis, Rastafarian gurus said, described a river in the Garden of Eden that flowed into four parts. One of these was Gihon in Ethiopia. Hence, the Rastafarians concluded, Ethiopia was the location of the Garden of Eden, the heaven on Earth to which all Black people would one day return.

All that was needed was the message from the messiah. The messiah, it was decided, was Haile Selassie, emperor of Ethiopia from 1930 to 1974. Before he ascended the throne, he was Ras (Prince) Tafari Makonnen. The cult borrowed the would-be prophet's name, eulogizing him with titles like 'Lion of Judah' and 'King of Zion'. For them, Haile Selassie was 225th in the Solomonic line, descended from King Solomon and the Queen of Sheba.

The Rastafarian creed was a Judeo-Christian amalgam, hailing both the Cross and the Star of David. Of its converts, Bob Marley, the reggae star, was perhaps the best known. Haile Selassie, however, remained unconvinced by a faith founded in his name. When a group of Rastafarians visited Ethiopia to greet him, an official showed them the way out of the imperial palace. The messiah refused to recognize his own disciples!

FACING PAGE: King Ras Tafari seated at the reception table after his coronation.

Coca-Cola
DEAR
SANTA
PLEASE
PAUSE
HERE.
JIMMY.
Good
Boys
&
Girls

Santa is a Coke bottle

Is Santa Claus' trademark red and white get-up a Coca-Cola invention? Before the cola giant appropriated the familiar Christmas-time figure for its promotional campaigns in the 1930s, Santa Claus could as easily be spotted in red as in blue, yellow or green. So what changed Santa forever?

The evolution of the modern Santa Claus is, like so much else in these global times, an American story. In 1804, the New York Historical Society was founded with St. Nicholas as its patron saint. A familiar martyr-figure traditionally associated with giving gifts, Nicholas was commemorated at an annual Historical Society dinner, to the singing of an old Dutch anthem 'Sinterklaas'. Somewhere along the line, the name was corrupted to Santa Claus.

There were many representations of Santa Claus: some saw him as an elf, others with almost sinister whiskers.

FACING PAGE: One of Coca Cola's earliest advertisements, showing their trademark rotund Santa Claus dressed in red and white.

Cartoonist Thomas Nast made a template image of Santa in the 1850s. Then came the Great Depression. In the 1930s, Coca-Cola wanted to boost a depressed winter market for its beverage and reach out to children too. It commissioned artist Haddon Sundblom to draw a prototypical Santa Claus, a large, guffawing man, with an easy, almost innocent demeanour. He was to be dressed in bright red, evoking the colour associated with Coca-Cola.

The all-new Santa was used by Coke on its billboards. In the pre-colour film (or television) era, it left its imprint. From now on Santa would only be red. Not because of an ancient Christmas ritual, but because of a modern marketing gimmick!

Coca-Cola itself is only willing to take half the credit. In 2006, it marked the seventy-fifth anniversary of Sundblom's contemporary rendition of Santa, but the company also insists that Father Christmas had appeared in red in images before that year.

Suicide cultists

Messianic leaders and charismatic loonies who take people to their death make for great Victorian scare stories. They also make up our world. On 18 November 1978, one man induced 914 people (276 of them children) to commit suicide. Most of them drank grape juice laced with cyanide. Some, it was said, were shot, others injected with poison.

Nobody will ever know precisely what happened. The 'Guyana Massacre', as it came to be called, took place deep in the jungles of that Caribbean island. Four thousand acres had been leased there by Jim Jones and his People's Temple to set up Jonestown, a sort of agricultural commune.

The People's Temple had migrated to Guyana after coming under scrutiny in its previous home in southern California. San Francisco journalists had begun to question Jones' faith-healing methods. He claimed to have a cure for cancer and heart disease. He certainly gripped the imagination of his followers, talking of an 'apostolic socialism' and, like all doomsday cultists, predicting the end of the world, in this case following nuclear war.

When Jones moved to Guyana, families of those who left with him were frantic. United States Congressman Leo J. Ryan, a Californian whose constituents had been afflicted by the Jones' frenzy, went down to Jonestown to investigate. A small group of 'disciples' decided to leave the People's Temple with him. At the airstrip they were attacked and Ryan was gunned down.

Fearing retaliation, Jones urged the residents of Jonestown to kill themselves, promising to meet them on

FACING PAGE: Dead bodies lie around the compound of the People's Temple cult after the over 900 members of the cult, led by Reverend Jim Jones, died by poisoning themselves; they were victims of the largest mass suicide in modern history.

Bodies of cultists lie around the 'throne' used by sect leader Jim Jones, above which hangs his chilling last message.

FACING PAGE: Reverend Jim Jones raises his fist in a black power salute while preaching.

another planet. When the decaying bodies were found before Jones' 'throne', the inscription above was only too chilling: 'Those who do not remember the past are condemned to repeat it.'

Repetition can indeed be tragic. The People's Temple horror was replayed on 19 April 1993, in a town called Waco, Texas. David Koresh and his Branch Davidian Cult – it was originally part of the Seventh Day Adventists but had broken away after a prediction that the world would end in 1959 proved to be false – set fire to their 'ranch, killing eighty-six Davidians in a mass suicide.

This, too, was a volatile doomsday group. It believed Armageddon was nigh. Koresh – he was born Vernon Howell but changed his name to honour the Biblical David as well as Cyrus (Koresh), the Babylonian king who sent the Jews back to Israel – lost his nerve and probably his cogitative coordinates when the Bureau of Alcohol, Tobacco and Firearms sought to serve the Branch Davidians a warrant on 28 February 1993.

Koresh responded with violence, he saw this as a sign that the world was ending. Even so, he was confused. As per his calculations, the world was to end in Jerusalem in 1995, not Waco in 1993. A fifty-one-day siege of the Branch Davidian Headquarters began. On that final day, when the Bureau sought to push through, Koresh retaliated by setting fire to the building, persuading eighty-five others to die with him.

The celestial fireworks

For centuries the people of the Scandinavian region knew of the great pyrotechnics in the sky, attributing them to spirits or even an enormous fox that lit celestial fires. Nevertheless, the Northern Lights have a more mundane scientific explanation.

Streams of energy-charged particles fly out of the sun every moment, some at speeds of 1,200 km per second. These particles collect to form solar winds, huge packets of solar energy. When solar winds collide with the Earth's magnetic field, some of the particles are trapped in the planet's upper atmosphere. When they meet the gases of the Ionosphere, the tryst is marked by a wondrous play of light and colour. Each auroral display generates a billion megawatts of electricity.

FACING PAGE: The sky looks surreal as myriad colours and shapes are formed during Aurora Borealis.

In AD 1619, Galileo Galilee coined the term 'Aurora Borealis' after Aurora, the Roman goddess of morning. He had the misconception that the auroras he saw were due to sunlight reflecting from the atmosphere. Up north in the Arctic region, this magic is known as Aurora Borealis. Down south near Antarctica, it is known as Aurora Australis or the Southern Lights. The Earth's population spread ensures that the Northern Lights have a greater audience and, therefore, earn greater renown. In Lapland, northern Finland, up to two hundred auroral experiences are reported every year. In the south of the country, you can see only twenty a year.

From Alaska to Aberdeen, Aurora Borealis are a fascinating phenomenon. Would it be possible to harness their energy? If it were, there would be no power outages in the world. Ever.

Super Ape: Is the Yeti for real?

To some it is the missing link, the Darwinian creature at the cusp of the ape's evolution to man. To others, it is simply the great legend of the Himalayas, the Abominable Snowman of the world's highest mountain range.

The name 'Yeti' derives from two words in the local Sherpa language: *yah* (rock) and *teh* (animal). For centuries the Sherpa people, who inhabit the highlands that straddle India and Nepal, have spoken in hush-hush tones of this gigantic creature living in the mountains, quick on its feet and blessed with the ability to make itself invisible.

In essence, the Yeti's mythology is no different from that of the creature known as Sasquatch to the Native Americans of north-western United States and as Bigfoot by the more modern residents of the region. Bigfoot's 'sightings' have been documented particularly in the past fifty years. There are claims that 'it' is eight feet tall, weighs five hundred pounds and can be adept at snatching children.

FACING PAGE: A boy looks up at a huge model of the creature known as the Yeti, during the shooting of Frank Kramer's film 'Yeti' in Rome.

Halfway across the world, contemporary theories of the Yeti go back to 1889 when, trekking in the Himalayas, a British army officer pointed out large footprints. In 1921, a 'credible' sighting was reported by a British team trying to conquer Mount Everest. At 17,000 feet, they reported a dark figure that disappeared almost as soon as it was seen. The experience of a Himalayan expedition in 1925 was exactly the same.

In 1938, a mountaineer blinded in a Himalayan snow-storm claimed to have been rescued by a man-like creature 'about nine feet tall'. In 1951, renowned mountaineer Eric Shipton took photographs of footprints in the snow. The Yeti's shoe size varied between twelve to eighteen inches.

It was the most authoritative 'proof' that the Abominable Snowman, as the Yeti had come to be known, was for real.

In 2003, a Japanese scholar concluded a decade-long research into the Yeti legend by concluding that, far from being the Super ape, it was no more than the rarely seen and almost extinct, Himalayan brown bear. He turned to language and etymology to bolster his case. Apparently a Sherpa dialect calls the brown bear the Meti, a word very easily corrupted to Yeti, the Japanese academic would have you believe. Similarly, Bigfoot in the American Rockies is sometimes thought to be merely a mountain gorilla.

Some would scoff at the idea. They would prefer to wait to meet the mysterious denizen of the mountains. To the believers, the Yeti is immortal.

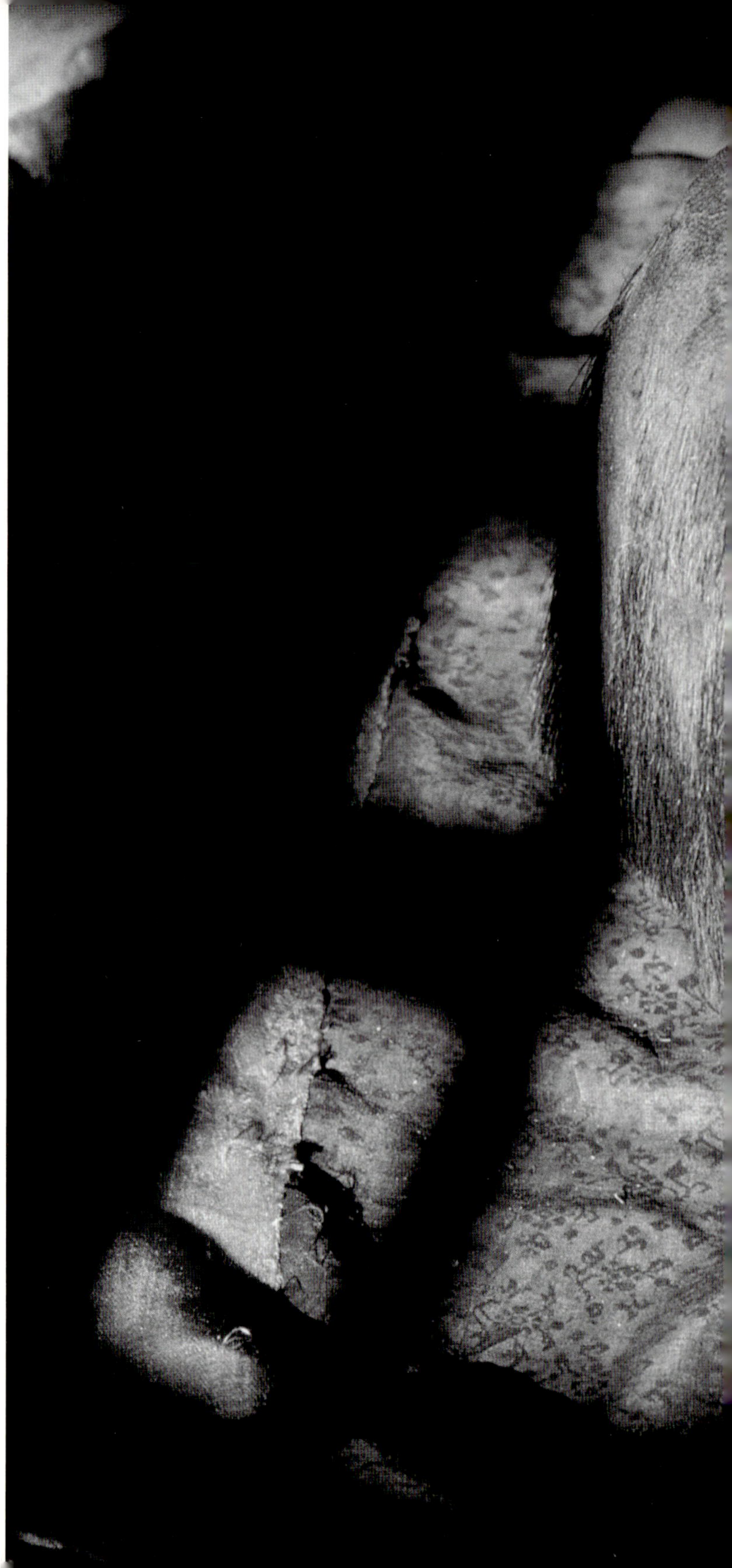

The alleged hand and scalp of a Yeti lay on a cloth in the Pangboche Monastery. Some skeptics and scientists believe that the hand came from a bear and the scalp from a goat's back.

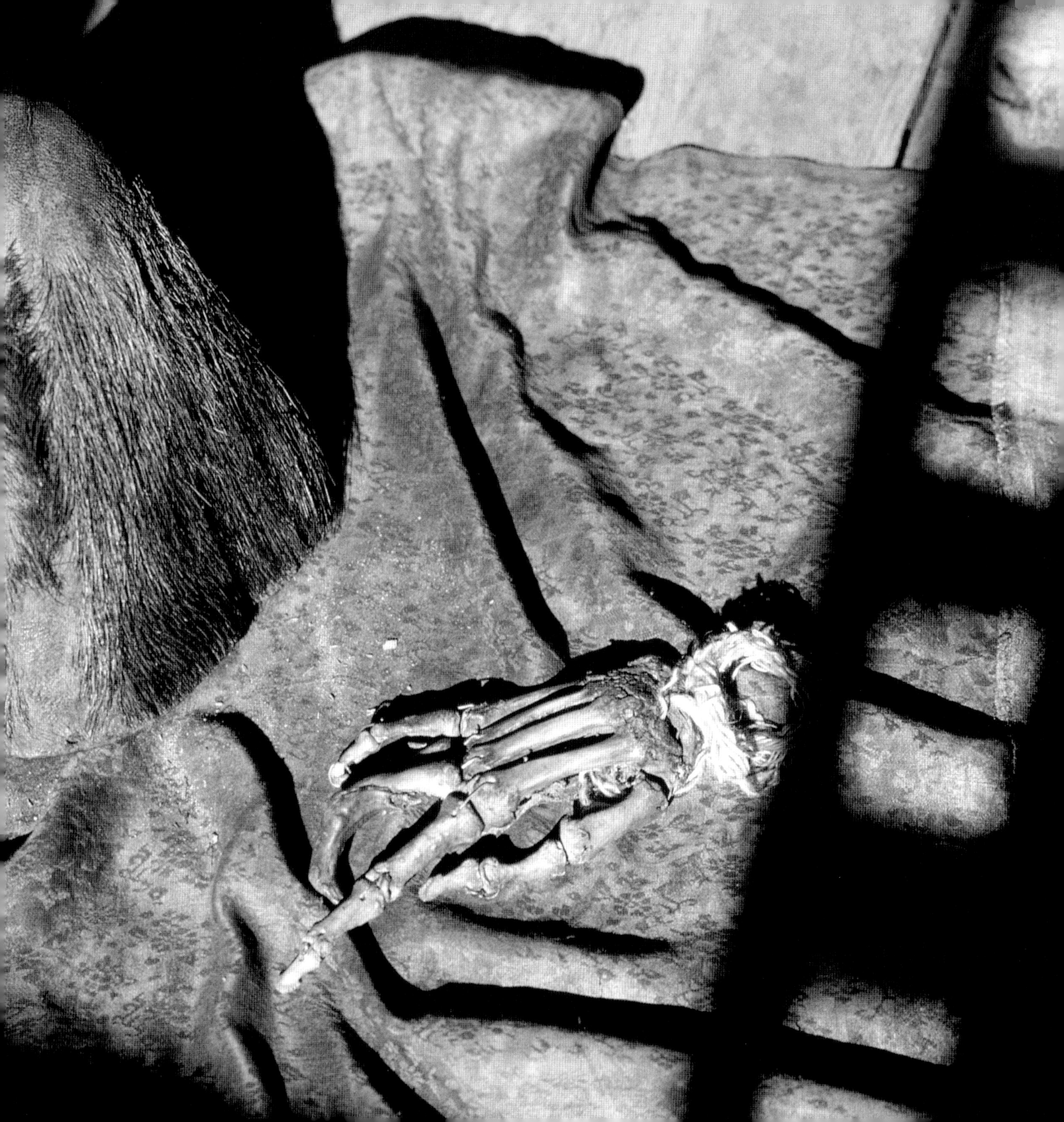

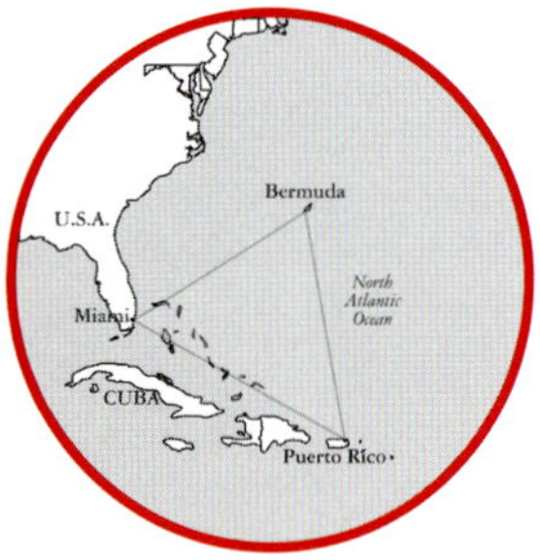

Triangle of terror

Right off the southeast coast of the United States, in a picture postcard location, lies the zone of death. The Bermuda Triangle is the world's most dreaded passageway. Its vertices are Miami, San Juan (Puerto Rico) and the island of Bermuda. Its calling card is mystery. In the twentieth century alone, some fifty ships and twenty planes are supposed to have vanished while sailing or flying in the Triangle.

The first recorded tragedy in the Bermuda Triangle goes back to 1780, when a ship called Saratoga went missing. In the modern age, alarm bells were set off by the disappearance of the ship Cyclops and the 306 people it was carrying. It remains perhaps the greatest unexplained maritime disaster in human history. It wasn't until the 1950s though, that the Devil's Triangle, the area's alternative name, acquired something of a cult following. This happened shortly after a clear day in 1945 when five United States Navy Avenger planes took off on a routine mission from their Florida base and were 'sucked' into the Bermuda Triangle. From then on, the Triangle became one of the most watched, most feared and most speculated about regions on the planet.

Theories about the Bermuda Triangle abound. Ufologists blame extra-terrestrial abduction. Others point to noxious methane gases emanating from the bed of the Atlantic. Still others see it as the setting of the 'lost' continent of Atlantis, which ancient Greek philosophers said had been swallowed by the sea.

The 'scientific' explanation is that the Bermuda Triangle is one of two places in the world where the compass points towards the earth's true north rather than magnetic north.

A reward poster at a marina in Florida for a yacht which went missing in the Bermuda Triangle in 1974.

Compasses usually point magnetic north, a variation of up to twenty degrees – depending on where you are on Earth – from true north. Navigators factor in this variation while planning their journey. At the Bermuda Triangle all this goes awry. The only other place where compasses point true north, is the 'Devil's Sea', just off Japan. Interestingly, it is also the site of numerous unexplained accidents.

According to some historians, even Christopher Columbus wrote of his ship's compass malfunctioning when he entered the Bermuda Triangle. The conclusion is that ships and planes lose their way, then swift sea currents sweep the debris away and no remains are found.

It all seems too pat for some people. If the compass goes askew, they argue, the planes should fly off-course. Why should they crash into the sea? The answer, is probably somewhere at the bottom of the Bermuda Triangle.

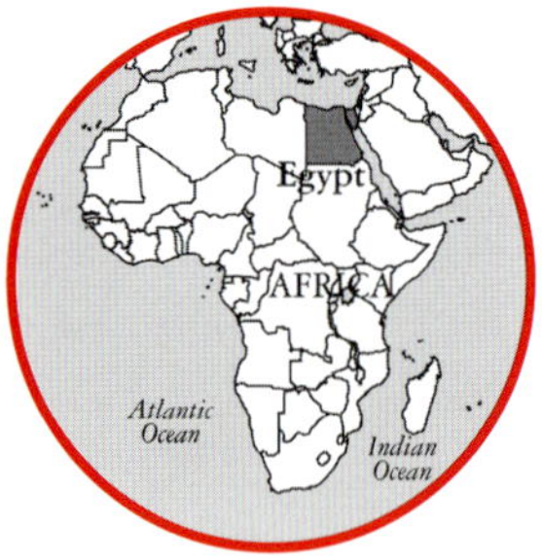

King Tut's curse

It lay undisturbed for 3,269 years, from the Pharaoh's death in 1346 BC to 17 February 1923. When the mummy of Tutankhamen, the boy-king of Egypt, was found amid the treasures of his burial room, it was one of the great discoveries of the modern age. With the discovery was born the legend of the 'Pharaoh's Curse'.

The tomb was actually uncovered by Egyptologist Howard Carter. On the day Tutankhamen's mummy was discovered, Carter's pet canary was devoured by a cobra. This was said to be a sign. The cobra depicted on Tutankhamen's head was expressing its displeasure, the murmurs went. The whispers grew into a fairly aggressive if wild speculation when Lord Carnarvon, who led the British expedition to find the remains of 'King Tut', died on 5 April, seven weeks after the mummy was found, of a mysterious mosquito bite. He was supposed to have uttered Tutankhamen's name in his dying minutes. The hotel room in Luxor that he was using when he died, has apparently not been opened for another guest since 1923.

The story goes, that at the moment the British aristocrat died, the lights went off in Cairo and, far away in Carnarvon's

Archaeologist Howard Carter (left) examining the intact mummy of fourteenth century Egyptian Pharaoh Tutankhamen.

King Tutankhamen's coffin made of gold, carnelian, rock crystal, obsidian and glass.

British estate, his dog howled and collapsed too, never to wake up again. The power cut and the dog's death could have been a coincidence but to the more imaginative, they were evidence of something sinister. That the jackal shrine found near the tomb's riches bore an inscription that swore to 'protect the deceased', only seemed to confirm the belief in the curse.

Within weeks of Carnarvon's death, his younger brother died, followed by the nurse who was looking after him. Next to go was Howard Carter's private secretary. According to one estimate, seventeen people somehow connected with the Tutankhamen find – or connected to those connected with the find – died in about two years. Other sources say six of the twenty-six people present when the tomb was formally opened died sudden deaths in the coming decade.

To this day, when the treasures of Tutankhamen tour the world, they carry the legend of the curse with them. In the 1970s, a San Francisco policeman developed a heart problem while guarding the Pharaoh's gold funerary mask. He sought compensation, blaming the curse for his condition. A disbelieving judge dismissed his claim. Wrapped in the mysteries of the past, Egypt's ancients must have smiled.

The Miracle Saint

Every year on 3 December, the Basilica of Bomb Jesus just outside Panaji in Goa, India, attracts thousands of pilgrims from the city, the rest of the country and the world. They come to commemorate the death anniversary of Saint Francis Xavier, the austere, scrupulously honest priest who is said to have converted a million people to the Catholic faith in Goa, southern India and southeast Asia before he died trying to enter China in 1552.

As incorruptible in death as in life, the miracle of Francis Xavier is his remarkably preserved body. To this day, the skin – without the use of artificial mummification methods – is visible as a parchment covering the body and his hair is there for all to see. To the believers, this is evidence of Xavier's holiness; to the rest, truth is stranger than fiction.

FACING PAGE: The body of St. Xavier, seen through a glass casket at the Basilica of Bom Jesus, Goa.

When the Spanish-born Xavier died on the Cantonese island of Sacian, his body was covered in lime before a perfunctory burial. The lime was meant to help his body decompose quickly, so that his bones could be carried to India. Ten weeks later, when the burial spot was dug up, Xavier's body was found intact. It was carried to modern day Kerala in southern India, and buried there. A year later, it was exhumed again and re-buried in Goa.

Over the centuries, parts of the body were cut off – some 'relics' were sent to the Vatican, others to the King in Lisbon, since Goa was ruled by the Portuguese. Each time the body was found incorrupt, soft to the touch with hair intact. One noblewoman is said to have bitten off the Saint's toe, only to find her mouth turn red with blood!

That last story is probably a myth. Yet, when the body was medically examined in 1951, doctors reported no foul smell, no sense of preservatives – four hundred years on, a relatively fresh body! Since the 1960s though, the legend has grown thinner, the skin is a little frayed, but still it scarcely resembles a body four centuries old. Every ten years, the Exposition of Saint Xavier takes place in Goa. The body is ritually taken out of its casement for the devout to behold. The next Exposition is in 2014. Be there for the miracle.

Every ten years, the body of St. Xavier is ritually brought out for devotees to behold. The next Exposition is to be held in 2014.

The druids at Stonehenge

Every year in June, to mark the Summer solstice, a group of men and women in white form a circle around Stonehenge, sounding conch shells and invoking an ancient tradition. Britain, particularly England, has a reputation for eccentrics and plain crazies. Yet even by its lofty standards, the survival of the druidical cults into the twenty-first century is a matter of bemusement. To most ordinary people, the druids are only characters in Asterix adventure comics and in retellings of the Arthurian legend. They can scarcely be creatures of the here and now.

A druid was a member of the priestly and learned class in ancient Celtic society. They were suppressed by the Roman government and disappear from the written record by the second century CE.

So what explains the rituals at Stonehenge? To the believers, this is a remembrance of the 'real' Britain, the pre-Christian, pre-Roman, pre-Norman pagan culture of the British Isles. The linking of the dolmen configuration to Boadicea, a heroic Celtic figure who led her Iceni tribe in a valiant but doomed attempt to defeat the invading Romans, is a throwback to that pristine, almost mythical time.

There is no evidence to actually suggest Boadicea had the Stonehenge monument put in place. Even so, when has something as trivial as historical evidence disturbed

Burning torches illuminate the ancient Neolithic site of Stonehenge, as Druids gather for the summer solstice.

believers? Perhaps the most famous Stonehenge myth – it can be dated back to at least twelfth century accounts – says that the structure stands at the site of a burial ground, where three hundred Celtic warriors were slain by a Saxon army. The local king – according to some sources, Uther Pendragon, father of Arthur – then decided to build a martyr's memorial.

Uther was directed to an array of massive stones in Ireland called the Giant's Ring, said to have been put together by visitors from Africa in some pre-historical age. The Giant's Ring was transported to the Salisbury Plain and became Stonehenge. Others see Stonehenge as a sign of alien visitors, an arrangement of some astral significance.

The origins of Stonehenge may be debated and fantasized about. What is clearer is the purpose it serves. Worship of dolmen or menhir structures and ceremonies at stone circles were not unknown in pre-Christian Britain and France. To these Celtics, druids were not just priests. They were the intellectual class, men of God, astrologers, judges, counsellors.

Stonehenge was not put in place at one go. The earliest stones go back to 2000 BC but revisions and embellishments continued over the next two millennia. While it is unclear whether it was associated with death, at least four skeletons have been found here. One of them indicated death by execution, leading to speculation that Stonehenge, at some stage, was a place to punish criminals.

Right now, it's the summertime meeting ground for post-modern druids.

Who stole Charlie?

In just so many ways, the 'Mystery of the Kidnapped Body' was a fitting finale to Chaplin's career. Ever heard of a coffin being dug up and kidnapped for ransom? It sounds like a strange joke, played, (in)appropriately enough, on the body of Charlie Chaplin, cinema's king of comic irony. Chaplin died on Christmas Day, 1977, and was buried two days later in Corsier-Sur-Vevey, a scenic cemetery not far from his house in Switzerland.

Just over two months later, two motor mechanics, one a Polish migrant, the other a Bulgarian, dug up the oak coffin and drove off with it. They hid it in a cornfield near Lake Geneva. Next they called Chaplin's family and demanded $600,000 to return the body, helpfully sending along a photograph of the casket to prove their credentials. They had

The endearing Charlie Chaplin brought laughter to millions worldwide.

Charlie Chaplin's stolen coffin which was found after eleven weeks following the arrest of two car mechanics in Lausanne. They were charged with attempted extortion and disturbing the dead.

got the idea for their little crime, they were later to confess, from an Italian film. Chaplin would probably have made a film on it himself!

As it happened, his widow Oona Chaplin refused to pay up, famously declaring: 'Charlie would have thought it ridiculous.' The exasperated kidnappers kept reducing their demand. They were eventually willing to settle for less than half of what they originally wanted. Meanwhile, police detectives began monitoring calls of suspects. Eventually, on 17 May they had their men – and the world got back its lovable tramp.

THE BRIEF CAREER OF THE LARGEST LINER

DESCRIBED IN THREE TABLEAUX

DEPARTURE —THE LEVIATHAN (AND HER COMMANDER, CAPTAIN SMITH) LEAVING SOUTHAMPTON— APRIL 10

DOOM —THE FATE OF THE TITANIC, ILLUSTRATED BY ICEBERGS FLOATING IN THE ATLANTIC— APRIL 14, 10.25 P.M.

DAILY GRAPHIC

ACCIDENT £1,000 INSURANCE

TUESDAY, APRIL 16, 1912.

TITANIC SUNK: APPALLING LOSS OF LIFE

DISTRESS —SCENES AT THE WHITE STAR OFFICES IN COCKSPUR STREET AND THE CITY— APRIL 15

Titanic replay prophesied

The Titanic disaster is one of those iconic events of our times. It reverberates and resonates in popular consciousness to this day. In 1987, an astrologer called Dennis Elwell realized that the planetary alignments for early March that year were exactly the same as they had been on the day the Titanic sank in April 1912.

Elwell wrote to shipping companies, warning of accidents. The letters were peremptorily dismissed. On 6 March 1987, The Herald of Free Enterprise capsized near Belgium, killing 188 people. It was owned by one of the companies Elwell had cautioned. The tragedy of the Titanic had undertaken another twist.

The 7,951 ton British car ferry, the Herald of Free Enterprise lies on its side, surrounded by rescue boats. Two hundred passengers died on the night of 6 March after the ferry capsized in waters off Belgium. The disaster happened so swiftly there wasn't time to send an SOS.

FACING PAGE: 1 May 1912: A newspaper montage of photographs and illustrations of the Titanic.

A view of the hole made
by a U.S. Army Bomber
flying in the fog which

9/11 precursor at the Empire State Building

'Airplane flies into New York's tallest building'. Sound familiar? It did, even back in 1945. Well before anyone had plotted the world's worst terrorist attack.

Between its inauguration in 1931 and the 1970s, the Empire State Building was the world's tallest such construction. That's when it lost its position as New York City's loftiest building to the World Trade Center, a title it was to regain in the tragic aftermath of 9/11. The Empire State Building is, without a doubt, the world's most famous skyscraper, featuring in ninety films, hosting the world's oldest vertical marathon and symbolizing the pinnacle of human achievement. Yet it hides a deep secret. Years ago, when it was only fourteen years old, a plane had crashed into the Empire State Building.

Saturday, 28 July 1945, was an unusually foggy morning in New York. A United States Army B-25 bomber was flying to Newark airport but lost its way and found itself in the heart of the city. Visibility was poor and to find an exit route, the pilot, Lt Colonel William Smith, began to fly dangerously low, skirting the skyscrapers of Manhattan, missing one or two of them narrowly. Suddenly William found himself facing the Empire State building. He tried to twist and climb but disaster was foretold. At 9.49 a.m., the plane crashed into the seventy-ninth floor. The B-25's fuel tank exploded, sending pillars of fire all the way down to the seventy-fifth floor.

Being a Saturday, the Empire State Building was busy. The World War II years, for many businesses had six-day weeks. Nevertheless, the freak accident didn't cause too many casualties. Fourteen people died, including some at their seventy-ninth floor office desks, and twenty-six others were injured.

One of the plane's engines did a roller-coaster journey from the seventy-ninth floor window to the roof of a neighbouring building. Part of the wreckage fell onto the street below. It took a million dollars to repair the damage done to the Empire State Building. New York, resilient as ever, shrugged its shoulders and went back to normal. Those were innocent days; nobody imagined a recurrence. Fifty-six years later two planes were to climb higher . . .

The Empire State Building ablaze shortly after a B-25 Bomber crashed into the east wall of the skyscraper on the morning of July 28th. Smoke and low-hanging fog shroud the giant structure.

FACING PAGE: The explosion rocked the building, showering debris over the area. Seen here, is a resident of Bronx beside a section of the ill-fated plane that landed in 33rd Street.

Divine rats

Rats are associated with filth and pestilence. However, in a little temple town in the Indian state of Rajasthan, they are worshipped. Nathdwara, near the historical city of Bikaner, is sacred to the devout as the location of the temple of Karni Mata or Mother Goddess Karni.

An idol of Karni Mata is the principal deity at the temple and keeping it company is a whole army of rats (called *kabas* by locals). Priests and pilgrims pay the rats homage, ensuring they are well fed – not surprisingly, some of the rats are even obese.

What is the spiritual significance of these rats? Legend has it that when one of her followers lost his young child, Karni Mata tried to snatch it back from death but failed. Angered, she swore that if anybody from her community died, his or her soul would temporarily reside within a rat, before migrating to a new human body and giving life to a new devotee of the saint figure. To worshippers at the temple, the rats are repositories of the souls of their ancestors, their dead family and friends. It is believed that if you see a white rat at Nathdwara, it is particularly auspicious.

Praying to animal forms is not unique to the Hindus of Nathdwara. The cow too, is a much revered creature in India. Nandi, the aide of the god Shiva, is a bull, making that animal holy too. Urban monkeys are a menace in some parts of India but devotees of the monkey-god Hanuman feed their simian neighbours and invite them home. Ganesh, the god of prosperity – a lucky charm for businessmen and new ventures – is half man and half elephant, and is accompanied by a rat wherever he travels. Sheshnag or the Serpent King is holy to those who pray to the god Vishnu. The expansive snake is supposed to be Vishnu's bed in the Ocean of Milk.

The rats at Nathdwara are clearly in divine company.

FACING PAGE: A man feeds rats at Nathdwara. Rats are sacred animals to worshippers at this Hindu temple.

The black stone of Mecca

Is the black stone of Mecca, one of Islam's holiest artefacts, a gift from outer space? About two million Muslims visit their religion's most venerated city in Saudi Arabia every year to perform the Hajj pilgrimage. The devout are enjoined to travel to the Kaaba – etymologically related to the word 'cube' and said to be so named because of its shape. The Kaaba is a large structure, the cornerstone of which is the black stone.

Hajj pilgrims are required to kiss the stone – only a small percentage of the millions who go actually manage that – or touch it or simply face it. Millions more face in the direction of the Stone – and of Mecca – five times a day, wherever they are in the world. This is the Muslim ritual of *namaaz* or prayer.

FACING PAGE: A time exposure photograph showing the whirlpool of movement created by devout Muslims performing the Tawaf, the circumambulation of the Kaaba, the climax of the Hajj pilgrimage.

The origins of the Kaaba and the Black Stone go back to well before the sixth century AD, when Prophet Mohammad founded the Islamic faith. Muslim theology believes the Stone was the site of an earlier temple built by Adam on his expulsion from the Garden of Eden. The Stone is said to have been given to Adam by God (Allah) himself.

The Kaaba monument, the belief goes, was rebuilt in later centuries by the prophet known to Christians as Abraham and to Muslims as Ibrahim. The black stone, Muslims believe, was originally white but darkened gradually, as it absorbed the sins of those who touched it. Historians say the Kaaba was a place of worship for the Arabs of Mecca well before Islam. The Quraysh tribe – to which Mohammad belonged – maintained it as a pagan temple, complete with 360 idols representing various streams of deism and animism.

Mohammad is said to have restored the Kaaba to the faith of Ibrahim/Abraham.

What other secret lies inside the Kaaba besides the black stone, now encased in gold? Nobody is sure. Non-Muslims are forbidden from visiting Mecca – the penalty is death – and other than the head priests of the city, the King of Saudi Arabia and chosen dignitaries, nobody is allowed inside the Kaaba. Scientists have speculated that the black stone resembles meteor fragments that have landed on earth. This may also explain the change in colour, they say. Meteors often darken after many years of landing.

So is the black stone the product of the asteroid belt between Mars and Jupiter? Only the heavens above can provide a conclusive answer.

The black stone put on the south east corner of the Kaaba is believed by Muslims to have descended from heaven as the symbol of the covenant between God and Adam, and Adam's progeny.

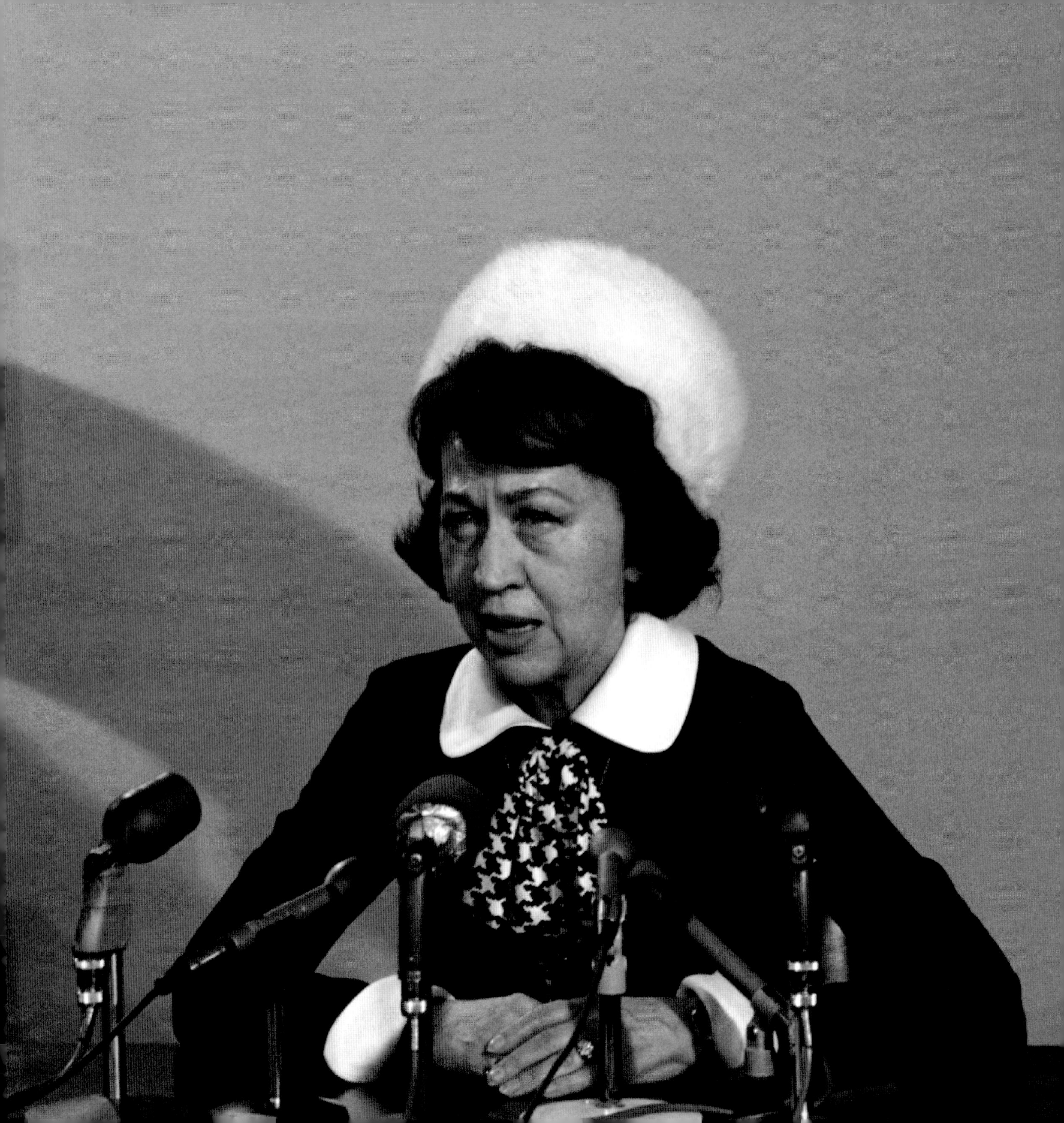

Washington's oracle

Since the beginning of time, man has relentlessly sought to know the future – astrology, the art of telling the future by studying astral charts, gazing at crystal balls, reading tea leaves, coffee grains, whatever. Few psychics and clairvoyants made as much news in the twentieth century as did Jeane Dixon, born in 1904 to German immigrants who had moved to Wisconsin in the American Midwest.

At the age of five, Jeane Pinckert – she took her husband's surname after marriage – met a Gypsy palm reader. The Gypsy woman told young Jeane's parents their little girl had the gift of prophecy. Her big moment was in 1956, when she informed Parade magazine that a Democrat would be elected president in 1960, but would probably be assassinated. When John F. Kennedy was indeed shot in 1963, Dixon's reputation as an oracle was established. She was anointed the 'Seeress of Washington'.

The legend of Jeane Dixon is unsurpassed by any western astrologer save Nostradamus. In 1945, she is supposed to have told an Indian official in Washington, the power-polis where she lived, that his country would be partitioned in June 1947. She was off by only two months. Six months before Mahatma Gandhi's death, she predicted his murder. She foretold Franklin Delano Roosevelt's death in the White House; the Sputnik launch of 1957, which began the Space Age; and Marilyn Monroe's mysterious death.

In 1968, Dixon delivered a talk at the Ambassador Hotel in Los Angeles and expressed her fear that Robert Kennedy, then a candidate for the presidency, may not live till the election. While leaving the room, she walked through a corridor and froze. She saw blood, she later explained, and

FACING PAGE: Jeane Dixon speaks at a press conference.

predicted Robert Kennedy would be killed just there. The Ambassador Hotel was the precise location of Kennedy's assassination a few months later.

In a 1978 tabloid she reportedly predicted that "a future president will be involved in misconduct around the year 1999"; indeed, it was in 1999 that Bill Clinton was embroiled and eventually impeached in the Monica Lewinsky scandal.

However, by the time she died in 1997, Dixon was seen as less an astrologer, more as an ageing if eccentric socialite. Political astrologers such as Joan Quigley, confidante of Nancy Reagan and the invisible hand guiding Ronald Reagan's term in office, had long superseded her. Jeane Dixon had her sceptics. Many pointed out that four years after the Parade article, on the eve of the 1960 election, she categorically announced John F. Kennedy would lose. In 1968, the year she foresaw Robert Kennedy's killing, she confidently refuted claims that Jacqueline Kennedy – JFK's widow – would remarry. The next day Jackie Kennedy announced her marriage to shipping tycoon Aristotle Onassis.

Critics say Dixon was more wrong than right. They even coined the term 'Jeane Dixon Effect' implying the propensity of the media to highlight correct predictions of psychics and soothsayers, suppress their failures and create an overstated impression of their abilities.

Perhaps the most eerie, most bizarre moment of Dixon's life came on the morning of 5 February 1962. For two days prior to that, she had been seeing strange lights and spherical balls at her Washington home. At dawn on 5 February she said she saw a dazzling sun, out of which stepped Queen Nefertiti, perhaps the most beautiful woman in ancient Egypt, with a newborn babe. Dixon's vision and her perception of it told her that a child had been born in the Middle East that day. In the coming half-century, he would exert a remarkable influence on the world. Like so much else about Dixon, the nature of this influence, negative or positive, was left ambiguous.

Who is this man? Is he the next sinister terrorist, lurking in the shadows? Is he the wise soul who will finally lead the Arab world out of its turbulence? Wherever she is, Jeane Dixon must know.

FACING PAGE: Noted psychic Jeane Dixon holding a crystal ball.

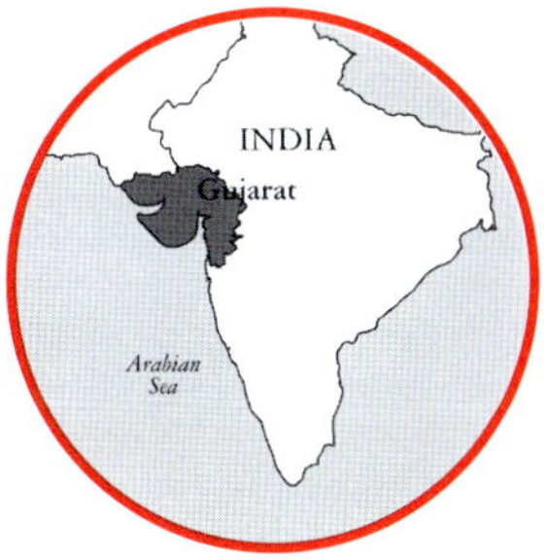

Prince among dogs

Lifestyles of the rich and famous are the stuff of eternal fascination, bringing out the voyeur in us all. Few of the idle wealthy lived in the pomp and style, and utter decadence, of the 550-odd maharajas or princes who ruled small kingdoms under the larger ambit of British India. By the mid-twentieth century, the Nawab of Junagadh, Mahabat Khan Rasul Khan, was more than just a ruler of a small state in a western corner of India. He was the world's ultimate dog lover. The Nawab's retinue comprised eight hundred canines, each with a room, a shampoo and perfume equipped bathroom, a telephone and a personal attendant.

When the Nawab invited the British viceroy to the wedding of Roshanara and Bobby, the imperial representative had no option but to refuse. He was unsure whether this was an insult or an honour. Roshanara, after all, was the Nawab's pet bitch, and Bobby the golden retriever of a neighbouring prince.

The wedding was opulence personified. 'Bridegroom' Bobby was received by a military band, a guard of honour and a regiment of two hundred and fifty dogs dressed in brocade. Roshanara arrived for the wedding ceremony in a silver palanquin. Bobby was endowed with glittering gold jewels.

The Nawab's love for his dogs was absolute. He took them with him on holidays, parading down the street of a bemused town with hundreds of dogs. When a royal dog died, its cortège travelled to the tunes of Chopin's Funeral March. A state mourning was declared.

That's one 'dog's life' no one would mind living!

FACING PAGE: The Nawab of Junagadh with one of his favourite dogs.

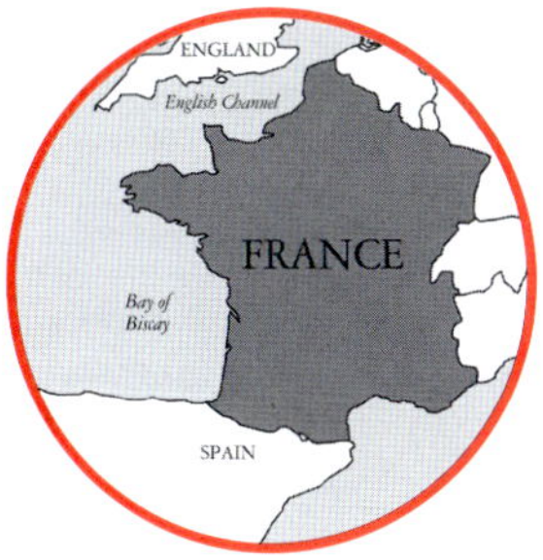

The rose that survived a war

'A rose is a rose by another name,' wrote William Shakespeare. Not if you listen to the story of the rose that is a rose by three names – Gioia or 'Joy' in Italy, Gloria Dei or 'Glory be to God' in German and simply 'Peace' in the United States. The rose in question was actually French – and it became famous for surviving World War II in an incredible, moving story of human effort and superhuman destiny.

It all began in 1939, when an international rose-growers' convention took place in France and at which Francois Meilland invited the delegates to his small rose farm in Tassin, near Lyons. It was a nice, pleasant day out

A catalogue for the Golden State rose, so named to commemorate Meilland's visit to California.

FACING PAGE: Francis Meilland admiring the Peace rose. "How strange to think," he later wrote in his diary, "that all these millions of rosebushes sprang from a tiny seed no bigger than the head of a pin – a seed we might so easily have overlooked or neglected in a moment of inattention, or which might have been relished as a tidbit by some hungry field mouse."

in the country. Meilland's guests were impressed by his labour, particularly by '3-35-40', the name given to a sample of roses he was experimenting with, having just produced them through a convoluted process of cross-pollination. For robustness, fragrance and beauty, 3-35-40 held much promise. Even so, it was still a work-in-progress. A German rose-grower concluded the session by suggesting the company gather again at the Meilland farm a year later to review 3-35-40's potential.

Three months later Germany invaded Poland and World War II engulfed Europe. A rose convention was on nobody's priority list. To the Meilland family, the war inched closer and closer. The Germans occupied France. It broke Francois' heart to burn down 200,000 rose bushes for the war effort. Every patch of green was needed to grow vegetables for sustenance, not flowers for indulgence.

Unwilling to see 3-35-40, his prized creation, just disappear, he sent a few buds to a friend in Italy, another packet to the German visitor who had hoped to come back. In 1942, as the last Allied plane left France, an American diplomat took a treasured sample of Meilland's rose for Conrad-Pyle, his agents in Pennsylvania. Three years passed.

FACING PAGE: Till date, five generations of the Meilland family have been cultivating their greatest passion, the rose. They name a few of their roses in honor of a notable person or celebrity, both historical and present day.

There was news from Italy: Gioia, as 3-35-40 had been renamed, was doing well. From Germany came good tidings about Gloria Dei. Only America, separated by an ocean and a titanic conflict, remained silent.

But actually, America had been very active. Meilland's American friends had tentatively named the rose after Francois' late mother, Claudia. The flower enthralled the country, from the East Coast to the Deep South. It withstood a variety of soil conditions, but looked and smelt as fresh as ever. On 29 April 1945, at an all-American rose-growers' ceremony in Pasadena, California, the rose that had enraptured a nation was re-named 'Peace' – in the hope that its resilience and grace would herald an end to warfare, that guns would fall silent before roses.

Coincidentally, a few hours later America received the news that Berlin had fallen. The Nazi army's last defence had fallen. In effect, World War II was over. The symbolism was simply irresistible. When the United Nations Charter was signed in San Francisco later in the summer of 1945, a Peace rose was presented to every delegate.

When the war ended, Peace was reunited with her French parent and Italian and German siblings. Today, it is believed that the original Meilland 3-35-40 is somehow related to almost every single rose in the world. Not unattainable for a rose that lived through a world war.

The fish that cures asthma

The wizened Celtic druids had their magic potions. The Native American medicine men had their mystery cures. The African witch doctors had their juju treatment. Medical science has rendered all of them out of work. Yet, deep in the back-alleys of Hyderabad, an old city in the south of India, a mysterious curative ritual is undertaken every year in early June, coinciding with the astronomically and astrologically auspicious Mrigasira Karti phase of the sun.

Tens of thousands of asthma patients from across India and abroad – travelling from Nigeria and New York, the Middle East and the Midlands – turn up at the residence of the Bathini Goud clan to receive a wonder medicine that will rid them of their debilitating respiratory condition. Special trains and buses are commandeered. Extra police presence is arranged to control teeming crowds and prevent stampedes. In the manner of an ancient prophet, dressed in a fresh white cotton dhoti and a saffron shawl, the patriarch of the clan distributes the medicine.

A little before they reach the house, patients are required to buy a small murrel fish, no more than about two inches long, and carry it in a clay bowl filled with water to the Bathini Goud patriarch. He places a yellowish paste – it is an ancient ayurvedic medicine, the recipe a secret with the family, passed down from generation to generation by word of mouth, never revealed, never documented – in the mouth of the fish. The patients are expected to swallow the fish live.

It is said the fish stays alive in the human body for fifteen minutes. In this period it gradually releases the

FACING PAGE: An Indian asthma patient S.Damodar prepares to receive a live murrel fish, stuffed with the secret concoction, at a camp organized by the Goud family in Bangalore, 2003.

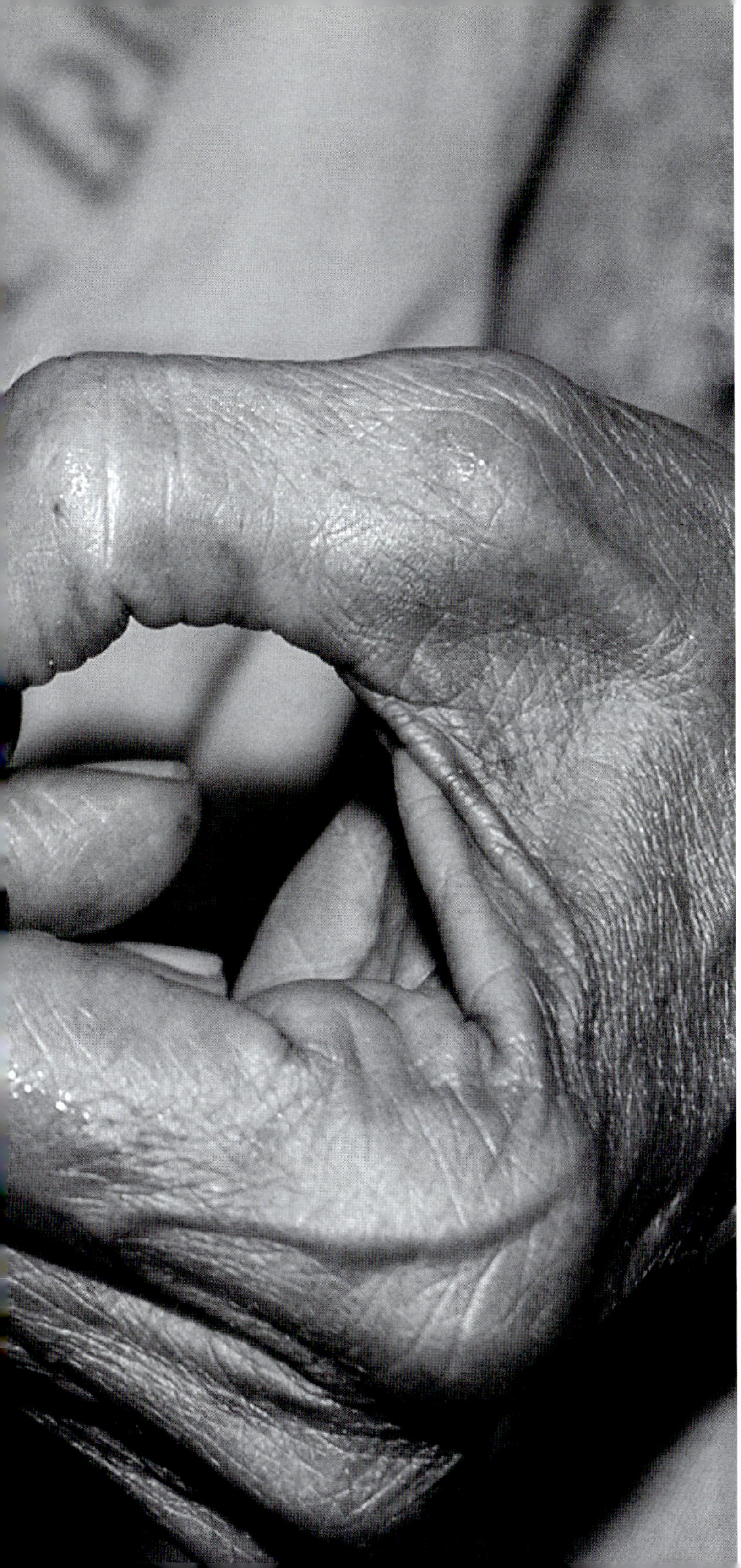

medicine, as it makes it way down from the oesophagus to the stomach. It is believed that acute asthmatics must take the full cure – repeating the therapy and gulping down the live fish four years in a row. Freedom from asthma, say the Bathini Gouds, is assured.

It was in 1845 that a sadhu, a holy man with healing powers, gave the secret to an ancestor of the Bathini Goud family. The sadhu had only one condition – the family must never profit from the medicinal recipe and must only give it away free. For over 150 years, the family has remained true to its vow.

To this day, despite pressure from doctors and scientists and sceptics, the Bathini Gouds have refused to divulge the ingredients of the paste. The family says it is afraid that pharmaceutical companies will reproduce it, sell it, make money from it – and therefore, albeit indirectly, cause the family to breach its promise to the wise sadhu from the middle of the nineteenth century.

Meanwhile, for the thousands who are cured of asthma – they are also required to maintain a special diet for the next 45 days – the secret of what is in the mouth of the fish doesn't matter. Literally and otherwise, they are content to breathe easily.

Bathini Harinath Goud inserts medicine into the mouth of a murrel fish before administering it to a patient in Hyderabad, 2007. The live fish, wagging its tail and fins, carries the medicine through the throat.

Idi Amin

Cannibalism is usually associated with ancient savages or horror movies. On rare occasions, normal, completely everyday people too are forced to resort to it. In 1972, survivors of an air crash had to live through harrowing conditions high in the Chilean Andes till rescuers arrived. They were compelled to eat the flesh of dead co-passengers. Such extreme examples notwithstanding, cannibalism is not quite a meal of choice.

Longtime watchers of Dada Idi Amin may disagree. In 1971, Amin, then army general of Uganda, became the dictator of his African country courtesy a coup. Thus began one of the most grotesquely colourful autocracies in the history of man, comparable to Herod, Caligula, Atilla; you name it. Amin, like many of his predecessors, had a penchant for the death penalty. Opponents were shot or beheaded. Some were singled out for special posthumous attention – their heads found place on Amin's dining table, the general upbraiding them while he ate. Dinner itself sometimes comprised a dead rival's heart, it was said in Uganda, cut up and tucked away in Amin's deep freezer.

Amin, forty-six and a former Ugandan heavyweight boxing champion when he usurped power, had many chips on his broad (well, with his weight at 110 kgs, they must have been broad) shoulders. When not dining heartily, he was known to interrupt pool parties by jumping into the water in full military regalia or, according to some reports, watch while political prisoners clubbed each other to death. The ancient Romans had just the word for such a scene – they called it the 'Circus'.

Amin had the most original views about history, geography and sociology. He frequently threatened

FACING PAGE: Rumours of Idi Amin's cannibalistic tendencies abound.

neighbouring countries, claiming their territory on the basis of tribal oral tradition. He created the Order of the Mosquito, his regime's supreme honour, named after the creature he said forced the British Empire out of Africa. In 1978, having driven his citizens to death or exile and his country to waste, Amin invaded Tanzania. It backfired. He was soon defeated and exiled to Saudi Arabia.

No more hearts for Mr Amin. He had bitten off more than he could chew.

ABOVE: President Idi Amin is carried by four Britons into official reception on a makeshift throne. It was Amin's idea, a way of showing the new white man's burden in Africa, and improving relations between Britain and Uganda.
FACING PAGE: Fourteen whites, including a woman kneel before President Idi Amin and vow to fight against South Africa as they are sworn into the Ugandan Army.

The Japanese surrender ceremony taking place aboard the USS Missouri in Tokyo Bay, 1945.

When America 'flew' the wrong flag

Undoubtedly one of the modern world's best known visual symbols, the flag of the United States (sometimes called 'Stars and Stripes' or 'Old Glory') bears fifty stars, representing the fifty states that make up America. Yet one of the most striking and memorable photo-ops of the twentieth century depicts an American flag with only thirty-one stars.

On 2 September 1945, less than a month after warfare's first atom bombs annihilated Hiroshima and Nagasaki, Japan formally ended its role in World War II. It surrendered to the Allies, with the Pacific commander, General Douglas MacArthur accepting the defeated nation's legal capitulation. The ceremony took place on board the USS Missouri, or 'Big Mo', as the famous battleship was known. Photographs of the day show a framed American flag on the wall, while MacArthur makes his speech. The flag has thirty-one stars, not fifty!

The flag of the United States did have thirty-one stars at one stage, but that was a century earlier, when the number of states that formed the Union was only that many. Why was this bizarre anachronism permitted at such a moment? Who was responsible for this error? As it turned out, the presence of the thirty-one-star flag was deliberate. It had been especially flown in from the United States Naval Academy in Annapolis, Maryland, for the purpose of bearing witness to the surrender ceremony. The flag carried with it the weight of history. It was a link to the past, one of mixed memories for both the Americans and the Japanese.

For 250 years, since the seventeenth century, Japan had been a closed, feudal society. The shogun generals who ran it kept it away from the world, preventing 'evil' outside influence from violating it. Then, on 8 July 1853, Japan's

Y

destiny changed. Commodore Matthew C. Perry, a hardy fifty-nine-year-old naval veteran, sailed into Tokyo Bay with four warships. He broke through the silken curtain of isolation, his message resounding to the accompaniment of cannon fire. He came with a treaty from Washington DC: his president wanted Japan to become a trading partner, to open its doors, at gunpoint if necessary.

Perry landed on the shores of Japan with his country's flag, the first American flag to be unfurled on the soil of the Asian nation. His initial offer was rebuffed and so he came back again in 1854, with a bigger fleet and 1,600 men. It was a fait accompli. Japan had been forced into the world. Within five years, it had signed treaties with a slew of western powers. The 'Commodore Perry approach' became a byword for gunboat diplomacy.

To the American navy, the flag Perry took along with him – which flew on his flagship on that fateful voyage in 1853 – was a banner of change. It was this thirty-one-star flag that was preserved for posterity and recalled to preside over the surrender of Japan in 1945. Even the anchorage location of the Missouri was carefully chosen. It conformed to the anchorage coordinates of Perry's flagship, when it had come into Tokyo Bay (or Edo Bay, to use the Japanese capital's contemporary name) ninety-two years earlier.

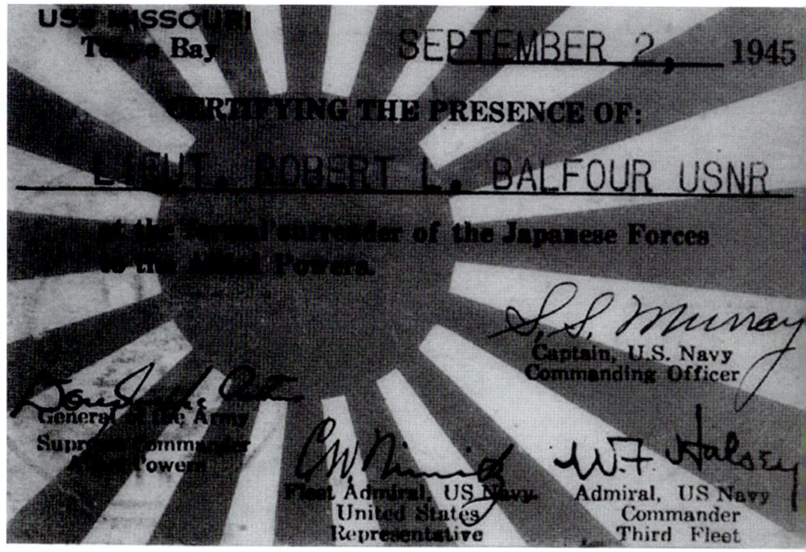

In a sense, General MacArthur's America had forced Japan's hand, caused it to cease warfare and, as things would turn out, embark on a path of economic reconstruction that would make it extremely wealthy. A century earlier, this was precisely what Commodore Perry's America had done. That thirty-one-star flag in a fifty-star era was only completing one of destiny's great circles.

ABOVE: Wallet card souvenir of the occasion, issued to Lieutenant Robert L. Balfour. These cards were issued to each man who was on board the USS Missouri when the surrender of Japan was formalised on her decks.
FACING PAGE: US Navy Admiral John F. Shafroth walks past the American flag, aboard the battleship USS Missouri, that was originally carried by Commodore Matthew Perry on an 1853 trade expedition to Japan.

The secret invasion of the bees

It's a fierce battle for territory across the Americas, and the African infiltrators are defeating, even decimating the European migrants. In decades, maybe years, there'll be no pure European left. Over the past decade, the invaders have begun threatening the United States itself, crossing over illegally from Mexico.

This is the story of America's secret war. It has its genesis in the Cold War era, a full five decades ago, and continues in a time of new turbulence. The war is not a human conflict; it is a tempestuous, life-and-death struggle in the fascinating universe of bees.

Bees came from Europe aboard explorer and settler ships in the sixteenth and seventeenth centuries. They thrived in North America but didn't quite take to warmer, tropical South America. Bees, of course, are essential to floriculture, primarily responsible for pollination. And the honey trade is another bee-driven business.

FACING PAGE: The African bee, known to be aggressive and a 'man-hater', is seen here perched on a grape.

In 1957, African bees were imported into Brazil in an attempt to introduce their genetic material that would make local (European) bees better honey producers. Instead of happily interbreeding, the two families of bees went to war. Being more aggressive than their rivals, victory was assured for the newcomers. African bees are twenty times as fast in terms of reaction time, eight times as lethal in stinging capacity in the first thirty seconds of attack. They are able to 'protect' longer distances – in other words, perceive danger from an animal or human being whom a more docile European bee may see as just too far away. They fight hard.

The experiment in Brazil ended up having catastrophic consequences. African bees began gradually but inexorably

moving north, crossing city after city, country after country. The African bee population made progress at the rate of 200-300 miles per year. All along the way, they destroyed the European-origin bees.

The African bees' battle tactics would do Attila the Hun proud. When they meet a European-American bee community, they launch a devastating attack on the queen. Once she is killed, her subjects surrender – or die. Within a short period, the host community is taken over, creating a hybrid family of Africanized bees. These are predominantly African, carrying only traces of their European ancestry, and very, very aggressive.

In 1988, the first African or Africanized bees entered Mexico. In three years, not one pure European bee was left alive. Mass extermination, genocide had found its equivalent in the society of bees.

Across the Rio Grande, lay the final frontier. In 1990, the first natural Africanized bee community was identified in the United States, living in Hidalgo, Texas. By the early 1990s, they had been found in New Mexico, Arizona and southern California as well. Movement up from the base, as it were, of the United States has been relatively slow. For one, ecological authorities have kept migration in check. The border patrol for the bee world has been facilitated by climate. The American heartland, the Midwest and the upper latitudes can get cold. African or even Africanized bees find it a bit too chilly.

FACING PAGE: An illustration showing the spread of the African honeybee from Africa to South America, to the USA. Brazil reports 300-400 human deaths a year caused by the bee, so severe and numerous are its stings. The pointed snout in the illustration is the bee's proboscis, used to gather nectar. The sting is located at the back of the body.

Why is the Africanization of bees a bad thing? Simply because, being more war-like in their disposition, they are known to target livestock, just fly off the handle and assault ordinary human beings. Many horrific attacks – including one in 1992, when a man who was only mowing his lawn was stung thousands of times and died a ghastly death – have been reported. In sixty years, African bees are said to have killed over a thousand people.

The aggression of the Africanized bees has to be seen in the context of the society they live in. In Africa, humans resort to bee-hunting and the 'aggressive' behaviour is actually 'defensive' action taken by the bees to protect themselves from human killers. In the Americas, bee-keeping is more common than bee-hunting, and hence local bees have evolved differently and learnt to respond differently to human presence.

All in all, the economic costs of that great bee flight of 1957 have still not been tabulated. Come to think of it, they may be incalculable, especially if the bees mutate enough to move up across the United States and threaten Canada as well. Not for the first time in history, one race would have wiped out another.

Names people play

In 2001, British author Fay Weldon wrote a taut, dramatic novel called 'The Bvlgari Connection'. The name of the Italian jewellery maker didn't make it to the title just by accident. Rather, Bvlgari paid Weldon an undisclosed sum of money to mention their brand name at least a dozen times in her novel. Eventually, Weldon wrote a piece of jewellery and a Bulgari store into her plot, mentioned the sponsor's name well over thirty times and produced what one wry observer described as 'commercial fiction'.

The book was meant to be a private circulation treat for Bvlgari's clients and business associates. Weldon liked her work so much, she decided to publish it as a 'normal' book, collecting an advance and royalties from Harper Collins, her publishers in Britain.

While advertising and brands are ubiquitous, their paid-for-use in a novel was certainly, well, novel. Even more singular perhaps was the case of Granville, a small North Dakota town that agreed, in 1998, to rename itself McGillicuddy City. The change of identity was, again, contracted for. Granville was paid $100,000 by the company that made the beverage Dr McGillicuddy's Schnapps. The money was used to build the town a new community centre.

It has, of course, been common to name products or brands after places. Nylon, the wonder plastic fibre, was said to have been named after New York and London, the two most important urban locales in the western world in the 1930s, when the polyester material was invented. In 2002, pop star Britney Spears opened a restaurant called Nyla – for New York (NY), the city where the eatery was located, and Lousiana (LA), the state Spears belonged to.

If Granville reversed the naming trend – a company lending its moniker to a city – in 2003, the strange notion entered the dotcom age too. That year Halfway, a tiny town in Oregon with a population of just over 350, voted to rename itself Half.com and began describing itself as the 'first dotcom city in America'. As it happened, the city council had been written out a cheque of $ 75,000 by www.half.com, an online book and CD store – later sold to eBay – that also gave away twenty-two computers to the local school.

Very soon, towns and cities will be bought over the counter too, perhaps auctioned online!

An exterior view of singer Britney Spears' new restaurant 'Nyla' in New York City.

Before the invention of celluloid, all billiard balls were made from ivory. Shown here, are what appear to be molds for the measurement of size.

Hollywood's billiard origins

As a base for photographic film and a veritable synonym for cinema, celluloid is one of those patented product names that has long since entered everyday language. For the first fifty years of the twentieth century, it was the wonder material of its age, as important to communication technology as, perhaps, the personal computer or fibre optics a few decades later.

It's almost unbelievable then, that celluloid began commercial life in the 1860s as raw material for billiard balls. Billiard balls were, at the time, made of ivory – expensive and rare. Elephants were being shot by hunters with a scary frequency, and only able to yield three or fours balls per elephant tusk.

Since money is the mother of ingenuity, somebody came up with the idea of a prize for the best substitute for ivory. A New York organization offered ten thousand dollars, which, a century and a half ago, was a very, very serious sum, for the invention of a new material for billiard balls. John Wesley Hyatt tweaked the composition of celluloid – a synthetic mix of camphor and nitrocellulose that had already been devised by an English chemist some years earlier – and earned himself the prize. He also won a patent for an artificial and theoretically endless resource for the production of billiard balls. Soon Hyatt was in business, setting up the Albany Billiard Ball Company to make celluloid balls.

As it happened, somebody soon discovered the multiple uses of celluloid. A clear material, it could easily have any colour injected into it. As such, it came to replace tortoise shell as a base for combs, buttons for fashionable shirts and by the 1920s, the material with which fountain pens were made. This was the beginning of the great plastics revolution. By the 1960s, celluloid was beginning to be seen as a crude

polymer, and was soon supplanted by its state-of-the-art successors. The billiard ball was being hit off the table by history's cue.

Today, the mention of celluloid is enough to evoke nostalgia for old movies and inter-war memorabilia. Guess what its most salient application is? It's used to make table tennis or ping pong balls. From one table to another, with a bit of Hollywood in between . . .

A craftsmen works on a machine, making billiard balls from ivory.

Why 1,400 tonnes of Spain is in South Carolina

In 1966, 1,400 tonnes of Spanish soil was shipped to the United States, packed in 200 litre drums, to its final destination at a riverside plant in South Carolina. This journey, from the Old World to the New, mirroring the Age of Discovery that Columbus had begun, hid a tragic and almost horrific secret.

On 17 January that year, an American nuclear bomber had collided with another American military aircraft 30,000 feet above the Spanish seaside location of Vera Playa. The bomber was carrying four devices, probably hydrogen bombs. The B-52 bomber eventually crashed into the village of Palomares. Three of the bombs were still in the aircraft. Miraculously, they didn't explode, though two of the devices were damaged enough to have their explosives contaminate the local agricultural land. The third bomb was found intact. The fourth was picked up eighty days later, 3,000 feet under the ocean. Local fisherman had seen it floating in the waters before going down. American and allied ships began a search that stretched into a third month, anxiety levels not being helped by the fact that Soviet vessels conveniently entered the area to try and grab an enemy bomb if possible.

What had just occurred was potentially the gravest nuclear disaster of all time, a Chernobyl before its time. Yet it is hard to believe that today Vera Playa is a beach resort, a plush hotel standing at the location where the American government built a desalination plant for the farmers of Vera Playa. Access roads were built to the area. Annual medical tests for the residents of Palomares were announced, and are carried out to this day.

FACING PAGE: U.S. airmen scour rugged countryside for the missing nuclear device, during the fourth day of operation 'Broken Arrow'. The weapon was one of four on board a U.S. B-52 bomber which crashed in Spain.

Finally, of course, the contaminated Spanish countryside was uprooted, literally, and carried away to America. Undoing the 'Broken Arrow' incident – as the worst military nuclear accident in American history came to be known – was estimated to have cost the United States government fifty million dollars way back in 1966! Broken Arrow was, of course, kept under wraps at the time. Panic in Spain and the rest of Europe, fear among American citizens about the safety of the country's nuclear devices, the taut, almost paranoiac atmosphere of the Cold War: all of these came in the way of a full-fledged public admission of what had happened.

Why was the term 'Broken Arrow' chosen? The US Navy's definition of nuclear accidents listed Broken Arrow as an episode that, among other things, meant the 'seizure, theft or loss of a nuclear weapon or component (including jettisoning).' Other possible accidents were Nucflash – 'accidental' or 'unauthorized' detonation that could risk a full-scale nuclear war – Bent Spear, Dull Sword and Faded Giant. Thankfully, Broken Arrow is all the world has experienced so far. There has been no Bent Spear or Dull Sword, and no other accidental military nuclear nightmares.

U.S. Navy frogmen stand on the beach, preparing to search for the missing nuclear bomb; it was reportedly found lying in 200 fathoms of water.

2
89
89

The day the aliens came

Did alien pilots and their flying saucer crash into the Arizona desert in the summer of 1953? The testimony of three men, all far apart and all saying roughly the same thing, describing similar scenes envelops the most alluring UFO mystery of all time. To this day, the urban legend goes, the files related to the episode lie in the secret cabinets of the Federal Bureau of Investigation (FBI). J. Edgar Hoover, then director of the FBI, was said to have personally monitored the inquiry, and the cover-up.

So, what really happened on 20 May 1953 near the Arizonian desert town of Kingman? We pick up the story a day later. On 21 May, Arthur Stancil, an air force mechanical engineer working at an atomic testing site in Nevada, was called away for an urgent mission. He was being flown to Arizona, he was told, to ascertain the ground impact speed of a test vehicle that had recently crashed. The journey began uneventfully. Stancil and about fifteen other technical specialists took a military plane to Phoenix. At the airport, they were shepherded into a bus with blackened windows and drove four hours in a north-westerly direction. Early in this journey, Stancil – he was to break his silence over two decades later, in a sworn affidavit – realized this was no routine assignment. Their handlers told the fifteen people on the bus not to speak to each other, never mention what they were about to see.

Arriving at a location near Kingman, Stancil and the others were taken to a massive saucer, two convex plates fused against each other. The aircraft was about thirty feet in diameter, made of a silvery metal that seemed to resemble aluminium. Stancil did his tests and managed to peek inside

FACING PAGE: Hugh Marlowe and Joan Taylor walk below an alien spacecraft, in the poster for the 1956 film, Earth vs. The Flying Saucers.

the vehicle courtesy an open hatch. He saw what looked like an airplane cabin, complete with swivel seats. He also saw a chilling sight that was to stay with him till the day he died – the body of a humanoid, four feet tall, with brown skin, wearing a silver suit.

The next testimony came from a military guard at the Wright-Patterson air force base in Dayton, Ohio. He spoke of a night-time flight that brought in five crates from a crash site in the Arizona desert. Three of the crates, he was told, carried bodies of human-like creatures – hairless, brown-skinned and wearing one-piece suits.

In 1966, Ufologist Charles Wilhelm heard from a man who said his father had been at the Dayton air base that May night, and had told him the terrifying secret as he lay dying. This deathbed confessional was too strange to be fiction, he decided.

Did the United States government – rather, did the ultra-suspicious and careful Edgar Hoover, bury the secret? Was there fear that the country, still healing the wounds of World War II, and slowly getting embedded in the Cold War and the communist challenge, would react in panic to public reports of an alien landing, fear an invasion from the stars? Straight answers to these questions may forever be alien to us.

This man is one of the several people who claim to have spotted a UFO.
FACING PAGE: J. Edgar Hoover (1895 -1972) points his finger while speaking at a press conference.

The umbrella assassination

Caesar got the dagger, Kennedy the bullet: assassinations usually come with a limited choice of weapons. But Georgi Markov was murdered with an umbrella. The year was 1978, the city, London. Markov, a Bulgarian dissident against the communist dictatorships that ruled Eastern Europe and the Soviet Union, had been subjected to the most extraordinarily unique assassination in the history of the Cold War.

Playwright, novelist and, at the time, working as a journalist for BBC, Markov had been strongly critical in his assessment of the Bulgarian government. He was waiting at a London bus stop, when an umbrella pricked him. He instantly felt a pain in the back of his right leg, but limped to work. Within hours, he had fever and was in hospital. Three days later, he was dead.

Pathologists were initially flummoxed. It seemed like death by natural causes; well, almost. The reason soon emerged. Markov had been poisoned with ricin, a toxic derivative of beans of the castor plant. A pellet had probably been injected into his leg by a man passing by and carrying an umbrella. Ricin is so dangerous that it is listed in most modern security manuals as a weapon of mass destruction and a tool of biological warfare.

Who was Markov so dangerous for – that is, who murdered him? A dissident writer and thinker, Markov defected from Bulgaria to political asylum in the West in 1969. He began a series of radio shows – some of which could be heard by his fellow Bulgarians – that were scathing about the communist regime. The satire and bile was only augmented after 1977, when the government of strongman Todor Zhivkov refused Markov permission to visit his father, dying of cancer.

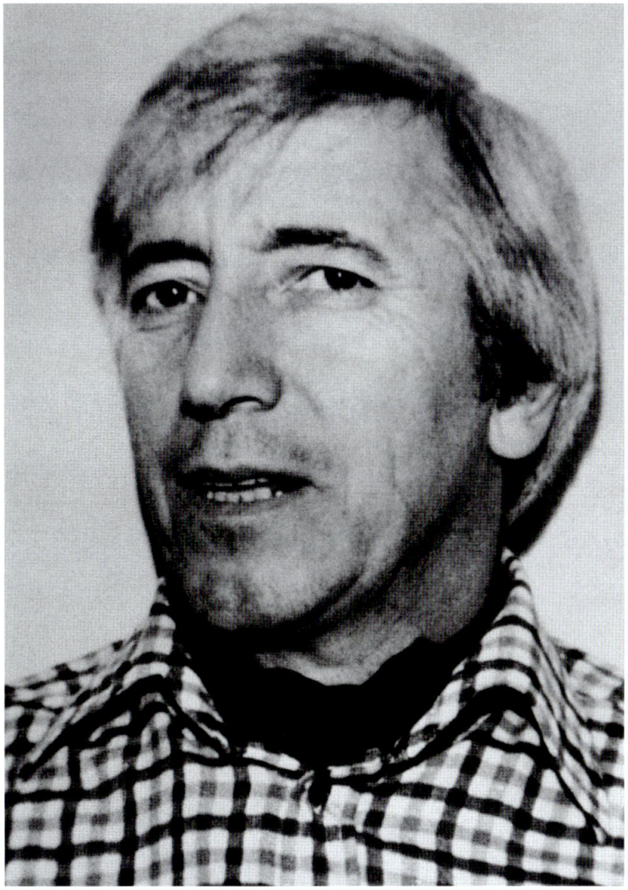

Bulgarian defector Georgia Markov was murdered when jabbed by a poison-tipped umbrella while waiting for a bus. Markov defected to England in 1969 fearing for his life after exposing sex scandals and corruption among Bulgarian Communist leaders.

Personal attacks on Zhivkov followed on Markov's radio shows. The enraged ruler wanted the humble rebel dead. A plan was hatched by the Bulgarians to murder him in London. The KGB – secret agency of the Soviet Union, provided the scientific and logistical support. It would be the perfect murder. Markov's death would be blamed on an immediate illness, it would seem natural. Ricin was, in that sense, a good poison to use, and an easy one to conceal.

A few determined doctors changed all that. The umbrella was in the dock, albeit metaphorically. Markov would have chuckled at the ingenuity of the plan. No one was formally charged with the assassination. A decade later, when the Soviet satellite states dropped down like nine-pins, western journalists and sleuths sought to bring Markov's murderers to justice. It was not to be. An uneasy alliance of black coincidences conspired against the dead dissident.

In 1992, the chief of the former Bulgarian secret police was imprisoned. His crime was that he had destroyed ten volumes of papers related to the Markov killing. An accomplice also suspected of shredding or burning r elevant documents committed suicide. A third spy, believed to have been on field duty in London during the assassination, died in a car accident.

As for the umbrella, it was never found.

Fatima and the power of 13

On Saturday, 2 April 2005, Pope John Paul II died, ending the most eventful and globally significant papacy since, perhaps, Urban II inspired the First Crusade in 1095. Less than two months earlier, in a convent in Portugal, another death had occurred. On 13 February 2005, Sister Lucia (Lucy) Dos Santos had passed away at the age of ninety-seven. The date was significant, for the number 13, so important to Christian theological symbolism since the Last Supper and the Crucifixion, had played an enormous role in her life. The two deaths were linked, it would seem, by some invisible thread, for Sister Lucy had been the inadvertent guide in John Paul II's search for his destiny.

Depending on how you see it, the mystery goes back twenty-four years – or eighty-eight years. Actually, both dates are milestones; the Secret of Fatima is, really, stretched across the twentieth century, into the morning of the twenty-first. On 13 May 1981, less than three years into his papacy, John Paul II was shot at in Rome by Mehmet Ali Agca, a Turkish youth suspected to be in the payroll of Bulgarian and Soviet agents. The head of the Catholic Church, Pope John Paul II – the moral force behind the anti-Moscow popular unrest growing in his native Poland – had been sucked into the Cold War.

The Pope survived and thanked the Virgin Mary for saving him. It was no ordinary thanksgiving; he had found the answer to a question that had nagged the Vatican for decades. 13 May was, after all, not just another date. It was the anniversary of the day in 1917 that the Virgin Mary had first appeared before three shepherd children – Lucy (then

FACING PAGE: 31st May 1952: A crowd of pilgrims watching the procession of the Papal Legate in Fatima, Portugal, where the Virgin Mary is said to have appeared to three children in 1917.

ten) and her cousins Francisco (ten) and Jacinta (seven). Looking after their sheep in the little Portuguese village of Fatima, about eighty miles north of Lisbon, the three children reported seeing a dazzling light, and a feminine figure. She promised to appear before them for the next six months, always at the same location, always on the 13th.

The first sighting became a local story; by the second, it had spread across the country. By 13 October, when the figure appeared before the children for the final time, a crowd of thousands had gathered, though only the children saw the figure. The sky had darkened that afternoon, and a storm seemed to be assailing Fatima. Eyewitnesses said the storm lifted fairly suddenly, and the sun shone with extraordinary splendour. Sceptics explained it as a solar eclipse.

Over her six visitations, the apparition is said to have revealed to the children three secrets. She is also reported to have to have told them that two of them would die soon. Indeed, within three years of the event, Francisco and Jacinta were felled by the influenza epidemic (the Spanish Flu) that shattered Europe. The deaths could be dismissed as coincidence, the Secret of Fatima was more difficult to rationalize.

RIGHT: Pope John Paul II prays before the statue of Virgin of Fatima in Fatima, where about a million believers attended the Procession of Candles. In 1997, the pope dedicated a shrine to Fatima, thanking her for intervening to save him from an assassination attempt in 1981.

A photograph taken in 1917 showing Lúcia Santos (middle), and her cousins Francisco and Jacinta Marto.

The first revelation came in the form of a 'vision of hell', of death and suffering. Jesus' mother, the children reported, told them that the war later called World War I – would soon be over. Yet if man did not remedy his ways, a second, even bloodier conflict was inevitable. Russia's secession from the Church was specifically mentioned. As it happened, the communists took over Russia in November 1917, World War I ended in 1918, but World War II began only twenty years later.

For decades, the third secret remained an enigma. Lucy, the surviving witness of Fatima, became a nun. She refused to speak publicly of the third vision. In 1944, she committed the description to paper, on the advice of the Bishop of Leiria, a religious figure she had regard for. In 1957, Sister Lucy's letter, sealed in an envelope, was delivered to the Secret Archives of the Vatican. She requested that the letter not be read before 1960, later explaining that she had an intuition it wouldn't be relevant before that year.

Successive Popes read the document, refused to tell the world Fatima's Third Secret, and returned the letter to the Archives. It was only in 2000 that the veil was removed. The third prophetic vision the children saw in 1917 showed a 'bishop in white', whom Lucy interpreted as the Pope, being gunned down near a cross.

The message was that the atheists ruling Russia would threaten the life of the Pope: '[Russia] will spread her errors throughout the world, causing wars and persecutions of the Church. The good will be martyred; the Holy Father will have much to suffer; various nations will be annihilated.' Yet the children were also assured of eventual triumph.

When Pope John Paul II was shot at on 13 May 1981,

Pope John Paul II with Sister Santa Maria Lucia; the latter, a 93-year old nun, is the only living witness to the Fatima miracle.

he knew the Secret of Fatima referred to him. Exactly a year later, on 13 May 1982, he visited Fatima as a pilgrim, prayed there, and gave a bullet Agca had fired at him as an offering. Today, the bullet is set in the crown of the Virgin Mary at the shrine in Fatima.

As the 1980s rolled on, the Catholic Church was instrumental in undermining the communist dictatorships in Eastern Europe. By the end of the decade, 'the atheists' had been defeated, church bells were ringing across former communist lands.

To think that three little children knew it all, those afternoons in Fatima, in 1917.

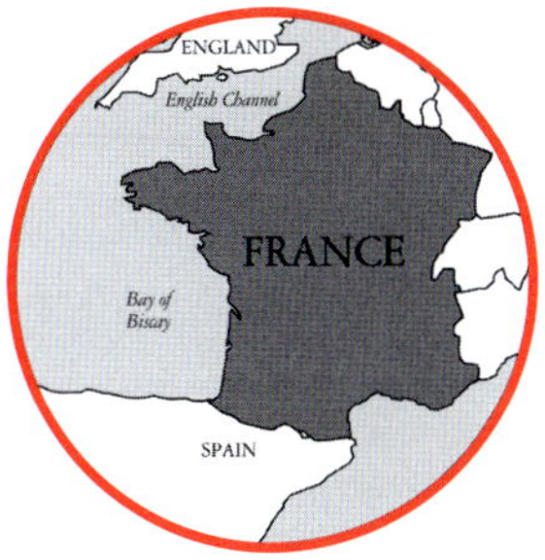

The longest non-divorce

Creative people live creative lives and make, if you permit the somewhat fatuous conclusion, creative lifestyle statements. When Pablo Picasso, arguably the greatest artist of the twentieth century, died in his adopted France, his death duties were paid to the French government in the form of his paintings. In his private life, he had married twice, made three women mothers and produced four children. That rhythmic number sequence hid many angularities.

Picasso was, of course, more famous for his paintings, particularly for the haunting 'Guernica', depicting the German bombing of the Spanish town of that name during the Spanish Civil War. The painting was based on photographs taken by Dora Maar, a well-known figure in her own right and, by the mid-1930s, Picasso's lover – already the fifth 'serious' woman in his life.

FACING PAGE: Pablo Picasso and his wife Jacqueline wait at the Nice airport.

In 1918, at thirty-seven, Picasso married Olga Koklova, having walked out previously on two serious relationships and numerous shorter ones. Koklova, a ballerina, was Picasso's passport to Parisian high society. The two had a son, Paulo. Unfortunately, the wife was primness personified and the husband was a born bohemian. A clash was inevitable. In 1927, Picasso met teenaged Marie Therese Walter. Acquaintance blossomed into love, Picasso left Koklova and had a daughter, Maya, with Walter.

Marie Therese Walter kept waiting for Picasso to marry her, but the older, somewhat twisted man refused. French law required him to surrender half his wealth to his wife in case of a divorce, and he had no intention of giving Koklova fifty per cent of his money. So he waited and waited, till Olga died in

1955. At twenty-eight years, it was about the lengthiest separation in memory.

While Walter remained a constant – she was to hang herself after Picasso's death in 1973, still unmarried. Meanwhile the artist took on a series of lovers. Dora Maar was his wartime partner in the 1930s and 1940s. After the Allies freed Paris in 1945, Picasso celebrated liberation by commencing an affair with art student Francoise Gilot. They had two children, Claude and Paloma. Finally, Gilot left Picasso in 1953, fed up of his infidelity. It was the first time any woman had walked out on Picasso. He was bruised, they said.

Notwithstanding Walter and Gilot, he met and married, in 1961, ceramic artiste Jacqueline Roque. This marriage was more than that, it was an act of vengeance than acknowledgement of love. Though separated from Picasso, Gilot had wanted to legitimize their relationship and their children's identity. She arranged to divorce her husband and marry Picasso to ensure the legal status of her children.

Instead, soon after Gilot and Simon began their divorce proceedings, Picasso married Jacqueline Roque. He had his revenge on Gilot, didn't pay a cent in alimony to Koklova – never mind if the hapless Marie These Walter was left waiting at the altar. The Picasso script can't be beaten by any soap opera.

ABOVE: Spanish artist Pablo Picasso pictured with his wife Olga.
FACING PAGE: Pablo Picasso clinks glasses with Francoise, as they toast the artist's 70th birthday.

U.S. NAVY
U.S. NAVY
U.S. NAVY
U.S. NAVY
U.S. NAVY

John Campbell
Eddie Ryan
George Offerman
U.S. NAVY
U.S. NAVY

And the five died together

Even death is seldom so callous, it would seem, to claim five members of the same family on one day. It happened to the Sullivans of Waterloo, Iowa, during World War II. Five brothers of the family, aged between twenty and twenty-eight, were killed on a single day, in a single action. George, Francis, Joseph, Madison and Albert were a band of brothers, literally. Townspeople remembered them as good natured, and as close as brothers should be.

In 1941, the surprise Japanese attack on Pearl Harbour pulled the United States into the war. It also changed life for the Sullivan brothers. One of their friends, Bill Ball, was killed on the ship USS Arizona at Pearl Harbour. The brothers immediately gave up their jobs in a local meat-packing plant and enlisted in the United States Navy. Their country needed them; their friend's spirit was calling.

FACING PAGE: To bring the story of the five brave Sullivan brothers to the screen, 20th Century Fox Studio officials went to great extremes to find actors who resembled the original heroes. Pictured (top) are the five Sullivan brothers; left to right; Joseph, Frank, Al, Matt and George. Seen below are the actors who will brought their heroic story to the big screen.

Since the navy was short of men, it allowed the brothers to serve together aboard the USS Juneau. The Sullivans sailed together for the Pacific, about the best advertisement for America that a wartime nation could imagine. Then, eleven months later, tragedy struck.

Already damaged in battle, the Juneau was making for the naval base in the New Hebrides when it was torpedoed in the South Pacific, close to Guadalcanal. The ammunition store exploded, taking the ship with it. About a hundred men survived, six times the number who died. Among those killed were four Sullivan brothers. Only George, the oldest, was alive. He died a few days later, still injured, still at sea, attacked and torn to pieces by sharks.

Security concerns – and the fact that the enemy would get to know – came in the way of the US Navy publicly admitting the loss of Juneau and other ships. Back home in Waterloo, the Sullivan family stopped receiving letters from the boys. When survivors of the Juneau wrote to them, they clung to the hope that at least some of their five sons had escaped miraculously.

It took weeks for the dark, darkling confirmation. In January 1943 a Waterloo newspaper broke the news: all five Sullivans were gone. The Pope sent a message to the Catholic family, 'An entire nation shares your sorrow.' President Franklin Delano Roosevelt paid his condolences to Alleta and Tom Sullivan, the stoic parents. They were left with a daughter, and with Albert Sullivan's widow and his two-year-old son. The other brothers were unmarried.

The valorous brothers were an inspiration for America. In 1943, a naval ship was named for them. When it retired, another ship was given the Sullivan name, in 1997. In 1944, Hollywood paid tribute with a film, 'The Fighting Sullivans'.

Decades passed. James Sullivan, son of Albert, nephew of four war heroes, came of age. He moved inexorably towards his claiming his legacy – he too joined the US Navy. Never has courage donned such shining armour.

Mrs. Sullivan being honoured aboard the ship she christened USS The Sullivans in honor of her five sons. Her grandson, James Sullivan, 13, stands at her right and at the extreme left is Thomas F. Sullivan, father of the five heroes.

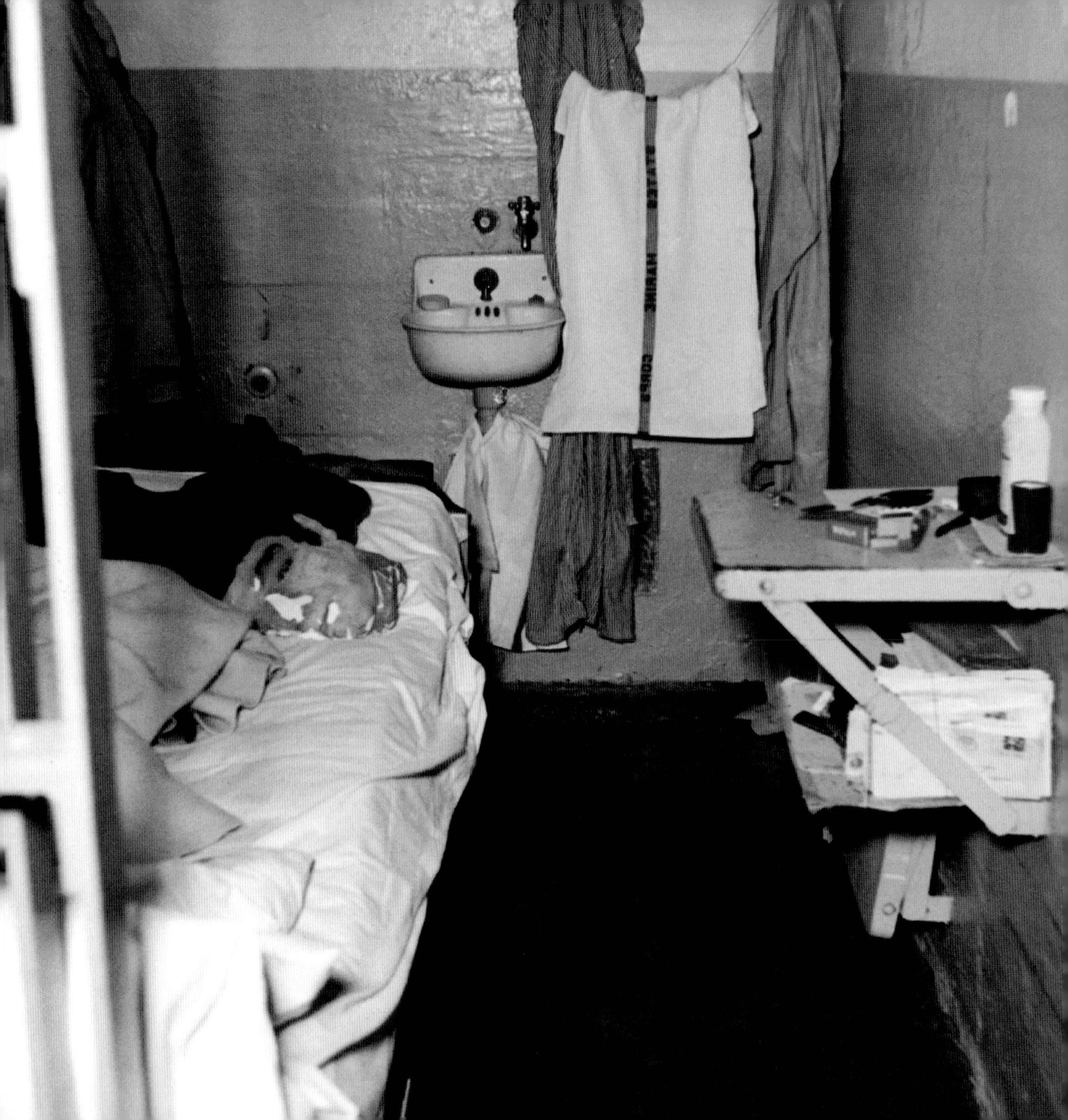

The Bay Area phantoms

Welcome to the most haunted prison on the planet. No visitor to San Francisco can miss it. In the middle of the eponymous bay stands 'the Rock', the formidable steel and concrete structure that was once the United States' – perhaps the world's – most redoubtable, least porous prison. Alcatraz or to give its full name, La Isla de los Alcatraces – Island of the Pelicans, the title Spanish explorers gave it, after they found its white colour was really a carpet of pelican droppings – was the United States' first coastal fort, a prison for a century from 1861. Today it is a tourist shrine and a sanctuary for ghosts and phantoms of prisoners long dead.

Long before the Europeans got to southern California, the Native American tribes of the area knew Alcatraz as a place of 'bad medicine', a lair for evil spirits. In 1861, still only a seven-year-old naval fortress, it became a prison for rebel soldiers of the American Civil War. During World War I, German POWs were brought to the island. In 1933, it was converted into a federal civilian prison, final home to criminals, murderers and every sort of American convict. This brought the eerie legend of Alcatraz into the world's view.

Alcatraz was a chilling, soul-crushing experience. No prisoner escaped alive, though serious attempts were made at least six times between 1906 and 1946. The most dreaded wing of the prison was 'D block' an underground network of fourteen cells, four feet by eight feet each. In particular, cells 9D to 14D were collectively nicknamed 'the Hole': no windows, only one dim light in the hallway, which was usually off, no excursion from solitary confinement hell other than for a ten-minute weekly shower.

FACING PAGE: This is one of the cells in Alcatraz Prison from which three prisoners escaped. Seen here is the entire cell, with method of concealing exit and dummy head used.

Mug shot of Al Capone in 1931, taken by the Chicago police immediately after his arrest. .

FACING PAGE: An aerial view of Alcatraz Island; the California coastline can be seen in the background.

This was the section where the most dreaded criminals were kept, tortured, starved . . . left to die. This is the section, it is said, their ghosts now haunt. Strange sounds have been heard at Alcatraz – metal doors clanging, prisoners screaming. Even the silences deliver a coarse message; the feeling that you're being watched is overwhelming, some say. The single most infamous cell in Alcatraz was 14D. Even today, visitors complain of an anxious, suffocating feeling, or a strange tingling sensation when they enter it. It is frightfully cold, twenty to thirty degrees below the neighbouring cells, though for no apparent reason. The partner in crime – two cells away – 12D is said to be home to a recalcitrant ghost who seems to hate company. Paranormal expert Richard Senate spent a night in 12D some years ago, and complained of icy fingers around his neck.

Cell 14D became notorious after a prisoner died inside it in the late nineteenth century – his spirit seems to be still pacing about. At least that's what the Alcatraz prison guard who found a dead body in 14D in the 1940s believed. The body was that of another prisoner. He had been screaming that he was being strangled by someone with 'red eyes'. The guard ignored the shrieking as he knew there was no other human in the cell. After many hours, the screams stopped. The prisoner had quietened down. The next morning he was found dead. A medical examination confirmed fingerprints on his neck. He had been throttled to death.

Alcatraz's most famous resident was Al Capone, the Chicago gangster brought to 'the Rock' in August 1934, sentenced for tax evasion. Prisoner number 85, as Capone was known, was guarded, like other prisoners, with machine guns. The cramped, cold and gloomy island-penitentiary must have seemed so different from the sunny vastness of the Midwestern landscape. Capone entertained himself, it is said, with music. Even now, people swear, late at night, when the rest of San Francisco is fast asleep, the sounds of Capone's banjo can be heard from his former cell in Alcatraz. This is one prison house that writes its own tunes.

A blonde Kalash girl dressed in traditional attire. The Kalash people have resisted outsiders for generations, and are some of the only non-Muslims in Northern Pakistan.

Lost soldiers of Alexander the Great

Close to the city of Chitral, in northern Pakistan, lives the last regiment of Alexander the Great's army. The Kalash people live in a valley region of that name. Some three thousand of them remain, residing in two hundred odd villages spread across the Barir, Bumburet and Rambur valleys, in Pakistan's Northwest Frontier, at the cusp of Afghanistan. This upland region is one of the final frontiers for human discovery. Well into the twenty-first century, it remains an enigma.

When Muslim rulers conquered Afghanistan and the part of India that became Pakistan, they named the Kalash country 'Kafiristan' (Territory of the Infidels). In the late nineteenth century, a local Muslim warlord tried to convert the Kalash to Islam, renaming the region 'Nuristan' (Territory of Enlightenment). Today, many of the Kalash have adopted Muslim-sounding names, but broadly guard their traditions. They are regarded as the last non-Islamic people in the Hindu Kush mountains, still practising a religion that is a mix of animism and ancestor worship.

Who are the Kalash? They say they came here from a homeland called 'Sym'. More authoritative accounts, and even their folklore, speak of them as descendants of Alexander's soldiers. The Greek conqueror invaded this area in 327 BC. He had just annexed the kingdom of Bactria (modern Afghanistan), where he had married Roxanne, the daughter of a local ruler. Now, the upper reaches of the Hindu Kush and the plains of the Punjab beckoned.

A year later, having won bloody battles against the Northwest tribesmen of the Indian subcontinent, and against Punjab's princes, Alexander's soldiers threw down their spears. They had marched 18,000 km from home, they were tired and wanted to turn back. The trek back to Greece was

a gruelling one. Apparently, some regiments lost their way in the treacherous, icy mountains. One of them ended up near Chitral, and decided to stay on. Their children became the Kalash community.

The similarities between the Kalash and the ancient Greeks were first authenticated by a British scholar in the 1890s. Like the Greeks, Kalash social traditions set great store by oracles. On festive days, they bring out grapes to please the gods. Grapes were associated with the Greek God Dionysius and used to honour him. As it were, Olympia, Alexander's mother, was a member of the Cult of Dionysius.

The Kalash are clearly of Caucasian stock. They have fair skin, blue eyes and blonde hair. There are etymological clues too. The Greeks worshipped Zeus and Aphrodite. Kalash mythology refers to Zeo and Frodait. Are they the same figures? Is Alexander the Great's regiment still waiting for him in an obscure corner of South Asia?

A Kalash teacher instructs children in traditional music at the Kalasadur School in the village of Brun. Built by the Greek Teachers NGO, the school aims to reinforce the indigenous culture of the Kalash people.

The curse of an ancient warrior

In 1941, Stalin sent a team from the Soviet Academy of Science in Moscow to the mystical, ancient city of Samarkand – then part of the USSR but now the second biggest urban centre in the Republic of Uzbekistan – on a secret mission: to explore the Gur-e Amir, the burial place of Timur, the fearsome fourteenth century Mongol conqueror known to the West as Tamerlane. Timur was believed to be buried with his treasures and his dazzling sword – said to confer immense power upon whoever wielded it. Timur's tomb had been kept a secret by his immediate successors, lest his enemies disturb his remains.

Led by the anthropologist Mikhail M. Gerasimov, the archaeologists and other scientists identified Timur's tomb and began to open it on 19 June 1941. So as not to arouse suspicion among the locals, they started work before dawn. They ignored a forbidding inscription above the tomb that read, 'He who disturbs my peace will unleash a scourge more terrible than I.' Early that morning, three old and mysterious figures appeared before the scientists. They urged them to stay their hand and return, not to violate the eternal peace of a conquering hero: 'Don't . . . or your country will suffer.'

After two days of digging, on 21 June, the excavators reached Timur's remains. The next day, 22 June 1941, Hitler invaded the Soviet Union. The most horrific war in Russia's history had begun. The curse of Timur had come true. The team brought back Timur's remains and some artefacts but could not find the sword. On the journey to Moscow, some of its members died in freak accidents, attacked by wild animals and the like. Timur's skeleton and that of Ulugh Beg,

FACING PAGE: An illustration of Timur, the great military leader who restored the former Mongol Empire of Genghis Khan, c. fourteenth century.

his grandson, were re-interred with full Islamic burial rites in 1942. On that same day, the Soviets won a major victory at Stalingrad.

In 1984, worried by the prolonged war in Afghanistan, Soviet president Konstanin Chernenko is said to have despatched another team to, officially, recover the bodies of those killed in the 1941 expedition and, unofficially, find the great Timur's sword. If the Muslim warrior's legendary weapon were found, the Soviets felt it would give them symbolic leverage in the Islamic world. Details of the mission lie buried in Communist-era archives in Moscow. They may never be found, much like the sword of Timur.

Gur-e Amir Mausoleum, built in 1404 for Asian conqueror Timur, is said to have inspired the Mughal tombs of Humayun in Delhi and the Taj Mahal in Agra.

The coup that stopped for gas

South America is no stranger to coups and attempted coups. In Bolivia, which became a republic in 1825, according to one reckoning, there have been 193 coups so far. Chile is another example; most famously in September 1973, President Salvador Allende was overthrown by the military.

Yet, just a few months before that, Allende, a charismatic if populist Marxist politician, had survived what must rank as the most bizarre coup attempted in history. In June, the activists of the rightwing political movement Patria y Libertad conspired with sympathetic army officers to kidnap the president and replace him. The plotters were such amateurs that, very soon, news of their conspiracy became public gossip in Santiago, the Chilean capital. As a result, the coup planned for 27 June 1973, had to be called off.

Plans were revived again on the morning of 29 June. Tanks and armoured cars commanded by Colonel Roberto Souper set off from their barracks in Santiago and made for Allende's residence. Inexplicably, they obeyed traffic lights – stopping at red, revving up and moving at green – and even took a break at a petrol station to fill fuel. Not surprisingly, the grand siege of the presidential palace – known as the Tanquetazo – petered out into a fiasco.

Yet, it had given others ideas. In two and a half months, a more decisive coup was mounted with the help of the US – and Allende was gone.

FACING PAGE: Chile's President, Marxist Salvador Allende, waves to the crowd en route to a military parade. The bodyguards surrounding Allende were chosen from party, not police ranks.

World best, but not Olympic record

As is customary at most multi-sports events today, some of the early competition at the Athens Olympics in 2004 got underway before the opening ceremony. A piquant situation arose when on 12 August, a day before the official opening of the Games, the South Koreans set a world record of 2030 points in the women's archery team event.

This was only a qualifier for pairing-off purposes, not for medals. Even so, the world record had been broken – but not the Olympic record. As per the Games' protocol, events conducted before the Olympic oath is taken at the opening ceremony do not count towards Olympic records.

The IOC adheres to this tradition because, as per its norms, athletes are only deemed to be participating in the Games after a representative of the participants has taken the Olympic oath and sworn to compete in accordance with the Olympic spirit. Never mind the world record!

The South Korean team displays their gold medals after the awards ceremony. FACING PAGE: Sung Hyun leads the South Korean women's archery team at the 2004 Athens Olympics.

BHOWAL CLAIMANT'S DEATH

CALCUTTA, Aug. 4 (delayed).—Kumar Ramendra Narayan Roy of Bhowal, whose 25-year legal fight to prove his identity was won in London only last Tuesday, died here last night, aged 62. He lived for only four days after the Judicial Committee of the Privy Council upheld his claim to be the second son of the late Raja of Bhowal, with a right to a large estate and a share in a yearly income of £100,000.

The law suit resulted from the Kumar's presumed death in Darjeeling in 1909, when his body, according to custom, was laid on a funeral pyre. A downpour of rain scattered the mourners. A few days later, having regained consciousness but lost his memory, he found himself among some Sannyasis (mendicants) and wandered about India as a beggar for 12 years before he recovered his memory. His wife, Srimati Bibhabati Devi, failed to recognize him and the legal action began, which culminated this year in her appeal to the Privy Council.—*Reuter*.

INDIAN TICHBORNE CASE

"DEAD" MAN'S REVIVAL ON FUNERAL PYRE

FROM OUR OWN CORRESPONDENT

CALCUTTA, AUG. 25

An Indian "Tichborne case," which opened at Dacca in November, 1933, concluded there yesterday with a result opposite from that of the English case. Judgment was given in favour of a *Sannyassi*, or *Yogi*, who claimed to be Kumar Ramendra Narayan Roy, second son of the late Raja Bahadur Rajendra Narayan Roy, of Bhowal, a wealthy landowner. He was awarded a third share of the property. His story the Judge said, did not rest on the credibility of witnesses alone, but was vindicated by every possible test. His bodily identity was proved with mathematical certainty by exceptional markings, and even if he had come back blind and deaf the conclusion would stand.

The plaintiff was thought to have died at Darjeeling in 1909, being (he alleged) the victim of a poisoning plot. When he was placed on the funeral pyre, a rainstorm broke and the funeral party ran for the nearest shelter a mile away, leaving the pyre unlit. The plaintiff awoke from his coma with his memory temporarily gone, and some passing holy men helped to revive him. He lived with them until 1922 as a disciple, and then returned to Calcutta and to his home at Dacca, where gradually many people began to recognize him. Eventually he brought a suit against his wife, her brother, and others who had benefited by his supposed death under the terms of his father's will. They all refused to recognize him.

The trial has involved 1,500 witnesses and large quantities of exhibits. The defendants produced a municipal record showing that no rain fell at Darjeeling on the date of the funeral. The plaintiff produced evidence that the record had been tampered with, and also that rain frequently fell on one side of Darjeeling and not on the other. Public opinion in Dacca has been with the plaintiff throughout the trial, and the verdict was tumultuously received. A daily newspaper was specially created at Dacca for reporting the case.

STRANGE FACTS OF INDIAN LAW CASE

The Judicial Committee of the Privy Council —Lord Maugham, Lord Russell of Killowen, Lord Romer, Lord Porter, and Sir George Rankin—yesterday granted the petition of Srimati Bibhabati Devi, a Rani of Bhowal, for special leave to appeal from a judgment of the High Court at Calcutta, dated November 25, 1940, declaring that the respondent, Kumar Ramendra Narayan Roy, was the second son of the late Raja Rajendra Narayan Roy of Bhowal and entitled to one-third of the properties left by him.

The respondent's case below was that he was the husband of the petitioner and that in 1909, while unconscious during illness, he was taken for dead and carried to the cremation ground, that after he had been placed by the funeral pyre there was a heavy rainstorm which drove his attendants to shelter, that he recovered consciousness and was taken away by sanyasis (mendicants) with whom, having lost his memory, he lived, wandering from district to district until, eventually about 1921, he recovered his memory and subsequently instituted the present proceedings.

The petitioner denied that the respondent was her husband, who, she said, had died in her presence on May 8, 1909, and had been cremated the following morning. She stated that the case concerned the ownership and devolution of property of very great value, and also affected her personal status.

INDIAN TICHBORNE CASE.

A REMARKABLE STORY.

(FROM OUR CORRESPONDENT.)

CALCUTTA, MARCH 29.

A case which bears a remarkable resemblance to the history of the Tichborne claimant is now being heard in the Dacca Court and is arousing intense local excitement.

A man known as Sannyasi appeared two years ago at Dacca and claimed to be the second Kumar Bhowal Ramendra Narayan Roy, who was reported to have died at Darjeeling in 1909. Both the civil surgeon and the Deputy-Commissioner at Darjeeling duly certified the death of the Kumar, but many who had known him, including some of his relatives, accept Sannyasi as the genuine claimant. I have seen photographs of both men and must testify to their extraordinary likeness. Friends of Sannyasi declare that a certain doctor poisoned the Kumar at Darjeeling in 1909 and then attempted to burn the body. Storms are alleged to have prevented the burning of the body, and the Kumar, recovering from the effects of the poison, eventually contrived to escape and to return home.

The physician in question has brought a suit for defamation against the friends of the claimant. Witnesses for the defence state that Sannyasi has the same wound and other marks on his body as had the Kumar.

Dead man walking

Can a man who's been dead a dozen years turn up alive? It did happen in India and as recently as 1921. The case of the Bhowal sanyasi made legal history, was the stuff of local scandal, and worldwide attention.

The mystery began in 1909. Kumar Ramendra Narayan Roy, second of three sons of Raja Rajendra Narayan Roy Bahadur, decided to take a holiday. He could afford to, as being the son and heir of one of the richest landowners of eastern India, he was entitled to a third of his father's property. The Bhowal estates were in the province of Bengal in undivided India. Today, they are to be found in Bangladesh, close to the national capital of Dhaka. Ramendra Narayan travelled with his entourage to Darjeeling, a hilly holiday locale overlooking the Himalayan range. There, quite suddenly he took ill, complained of excruciating abdominal pain – and died. He was diagnosed as having suffered a fatal bout of biliary colic.

FACING PAGE: Newspaper clippings from *The Times*, London, describing the infamous Bhowal Sanyasi case.

His body was ceremonially carried to the crematorium by associates and servants. On reaching, the group encountered a thunderstorm. It added to the aura of the moment; without warning, it was later said, the skies blackened and it began to pour. Leaving Ramendra Narayan's corpse on an unlit pyre, his friends sought shelter from the rain. They returned about an hour later, when the storm had receded. They found no body; Ramendra Narayan's corpse had vanished.

Twelve years later, a dishevelled monk (*sanyasi*, as the local Bengali/Hindi word goes) arrived in Dhaka and proclaimed himself to be Ramendra Narayan, heir to the fortune of Bhowal. He hadn't died in Darjeeling he said, hadn't even suffered biliary colic. Rather, an attempt had

been made to murder him by feeding him arsenic. He had lost consciousness and been thought dead.

Here the claimant's story became even more bizarre. When he was left on the pyre amid that storm, he said, a wandering party of Hindu monks chanced upon him. They found him breathing and sought to revive him by detoxifying his bodily system. They took him away to, as it appeared, safety and cure. Thereafter, due to the poison, the trauma of a near death, the betrayal of those who wanted to murder him, 'Ramendra Narayan' claimed he'd turned amnesiac. In this period he had become an itinerant holy man. As soon as he had recovered his memory and realised who he was, he had made for Bhowal – and so here he was.

Who had tried to murder the young aristocrat? The needle of suspicion seemed to point to his wife, Bibhabati Devi, who had inherited the wealth of the Bhowal clan. She refused to recognize the new arrival as her husband. The man who said he was Ramendra Narayan was certainly not welcome to share her property.

So the battle went to court. For nine years, the impostor or rightful heir (contemporary society was divided), tried to prove his credentials. He took his case to the local court in Dhaka. Bibhabati Devi told the court she believed this man was a fraud, his name was Sundardas Naga and he was the disciple of a senior monk from northern India. Some 1,500 witnesses were heard, 2,000 documents and photographs examined. Various means of identification were deployed. Fingerprints, which would have been clinching evidence, could not be used because no specimen of Ramendra Narayan's fingerprints from 1909 or earlier was available.

FACING PAGE: Three unknown *sanyasis* (holy men) from Northern India, 1910

In 1930, the court said it believed the ragged monk was indeed the aristocrat who had been thought of as dead. Bibhabati Devi appealed to the High Court in Calcutta. Here too the claimant won his case – Ramendra Narayan and the monk were deemed to be the same person. The resolute daughter-in-law of the Bhowal family then went to the Privy Council in London for one final appeal.

By now World War II had broken out. The planet was in turmoil. Yet for two people and the society they lived in, a property and identity dispute dominated all else. The Bhowal sanyasi case attracted press attention as far away as Europe. Finally, in July 1946, the Privy Council announced its decision. The verdict of the lower court was upheld. The monk was entitled to one-third of the Bhowal estate. Ramendra Narayan could come home.

Shortly afterwards, before the Privy Council's order could be put into effect and he could get his share of the inheritance, the monk died, of natural causes. The quarter-century long legal battle had taken its toll. In the estate of Bhowal, however, the lady of the house continued to insist he was not her husband.

Fruit vs. Vegetable

Is the tomato a fruit or a vegetable? It sounds like a quirky after-dinner quiz question. In reality, it was the subject of Nix vs. Hedden, a case argued before the Supreme Court of the United States. The kernel of the fruity problem lay in an 1883 tariff regulation that placed a ten per cent import duty on vegetables, but allowed fruit to be brought in duty-free. A New Yorker importing tomatoes from the West Indies was in a rage when customs officials asked him to pay up. The tomato was a vegetable, they said. It was a fruit, he insisted.

So on they went to the highest court in the country. In 1893, the Supreme Court finally made up its mind on which family to place the tomato in. Justice Horace Gray admitted that 'botanically speaking' the tomato was a fruit. It certainly was, and is: it has seeds and a fleshy pulp, about the best definition of a fruit there is.

The clinching argument for the good judge was that vegetables were eaten with the main course - 'usually served at dinner with the principal part of the repast' - while fruits formed the dessert. Since the tomato was not part of anybody's dessert and certainly not sweet, it could not be a fruit. As such, it was a vegetable and, if imported, liable to be taxed by the customs authorities.

Not surprisingly, domestic tomato producers in the United States were ecstatic. A rather unorthodox judicial verdict had fortified the walls of protectionism.

FACING PAGE: Whether the tomato is a fruit or vegetable is a hotly debated topic, even today.

Photo Credits

Coca-Cola, a registered trademark of The Coca-Cola Company: Page 30

Corbis: Pages 9, 12, 14, 18, 27, 28, 34, 35, 38, 40-41, 43, 50, 52, 56, 58, 59, 60, 63, 64-65, 82, 83, 84, 94, 96-97, 98, 100-101, 102, 116, 118, 122, 125, 126, 128-129, 132-133, 134

Getty Images: Pages 8, 10-11, 22-23, 24, 32, 53, 54, 55, 76, 78-79, 86, 93, 113, 110-11, 117, 124, 130, 136, 137, 140

Jacob Sonne: Page 20

Jeane Dixon Museum & Library: Page 68

Jean-Louis Nou: Page 46, 70

Library of Congress: 16-17, 87

M Anand/STS Images.com: Page 26

Meilland Pictures: Page 74, 75, 76

Nabanita Das: Page 90

National Geographic: Page 36

ISBN: 978-81-7436-690-0

This edition published in India by
Roli Books in arrangement
with Roli & Janssen BV
M-75, Greater Kailash II Market
New Delhi-110 048, India.
Ph: ++91-11-40682000, 29212271
Fax: ++91-11-29217185
E-mail: info@rolibooks.com
Website: www.rolibooks.com

Editor: Simar Puneet, Richa Burman

Photo Research: Simar Puneet

Maps: Nabanita Das

Design: Sneha Pamneja

Layout: Naresh L. Mondal

Production: Naresh Nigam & Rajiv Kumar

Printed and bound in China